15 Top Hits for Easy Piano

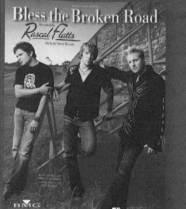

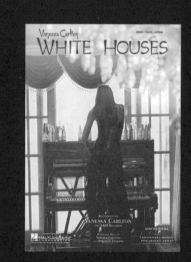

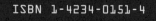

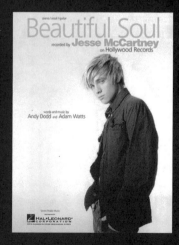

ISBN 1-4234-0151-4

HAL•LEONARD® CORPORATION
7777 W. BLUEMOUND RD. P.O. BOX 13819 MILWAUKEE, WI 53213

Visit Hal Leonard Online at
www.halleonard.com

Contents

BEAUTIFUL SOUL

Words and Music by ANDY DODD
and ADAM WATTS

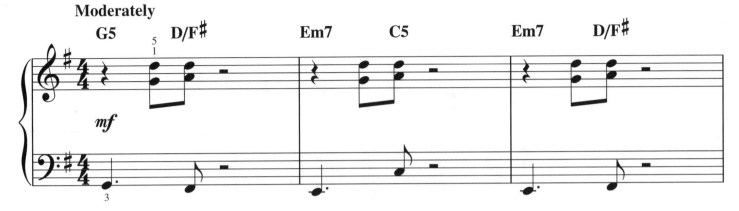

I don't want an-oth-er pret-ty face. I don't want just

an-y-one to hold. I don't want my love to go to waste. I want

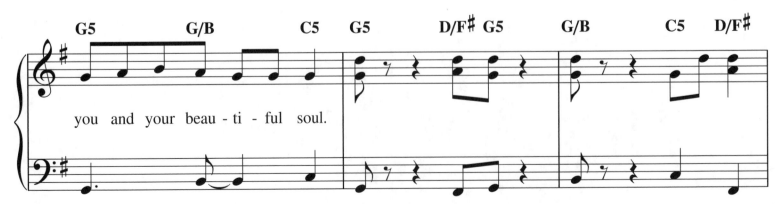

you and your beau-ti-ful soul.

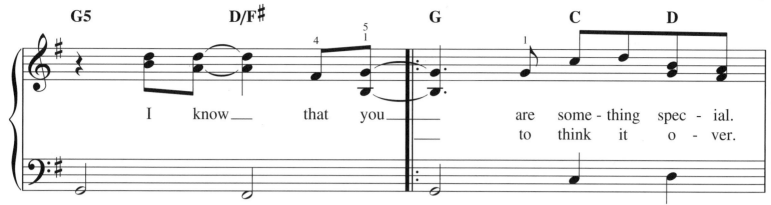

I know___ that you___ ___ are some - thing spec - ial.
to think it o - ver.

To you___ I'd be___ al - ways faith - ful.
But I'm___ just fine___ mov - ing for - ward.

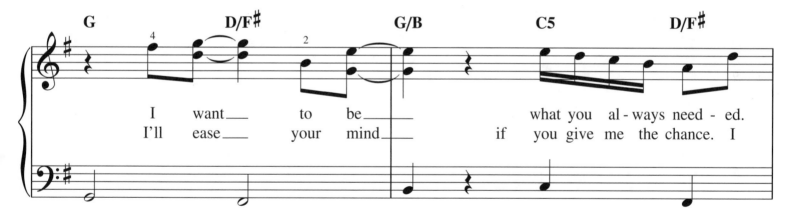

I want___ to be___ what you al - ways need - ed.
I'll ease___ your mind___ if you give me the chance. I

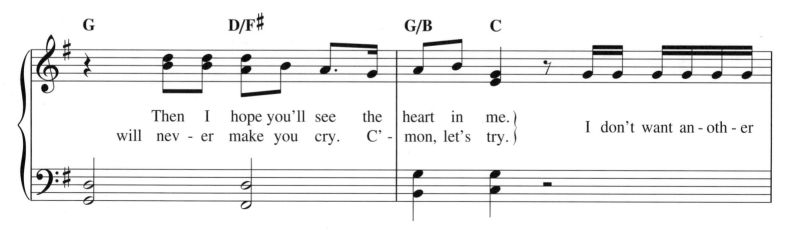

Then I hope you'll see the heart in me.) I don't want an - oth - er
will nev - er make you cry. C' - mon, let's try.)

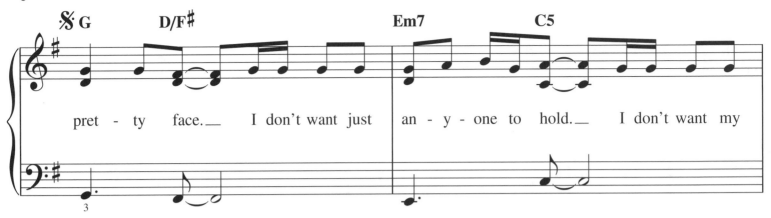

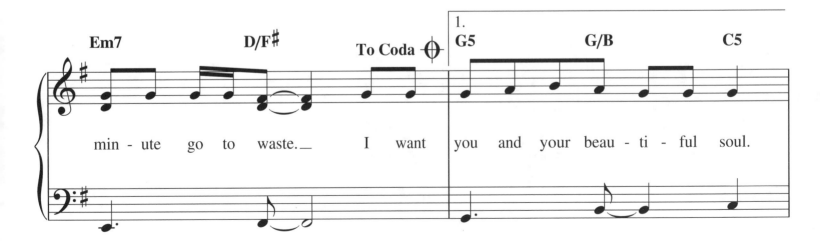

Your beau-ti-ful soul, ___

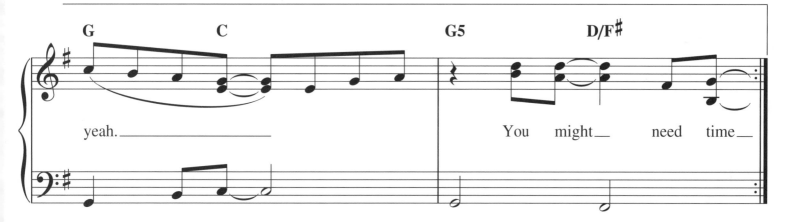

yeah. ___ You might ___ need time ___

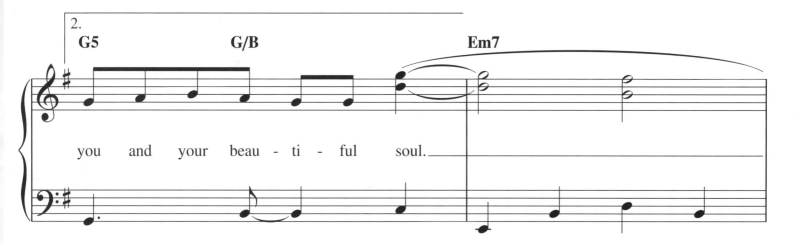

you and your beau-ti-ful soul. ___

Am I

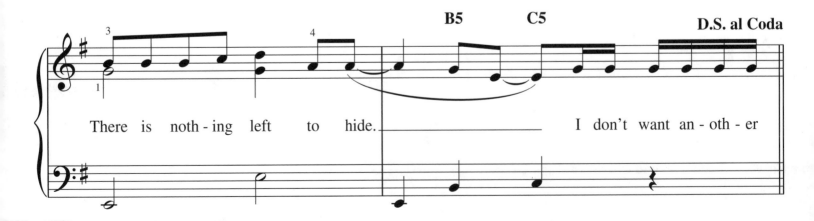

BREAKAWAY

Words and Music by BRIDGET BENENATE,
AVRIL LAVIGNE and MATTHEW GERRARD

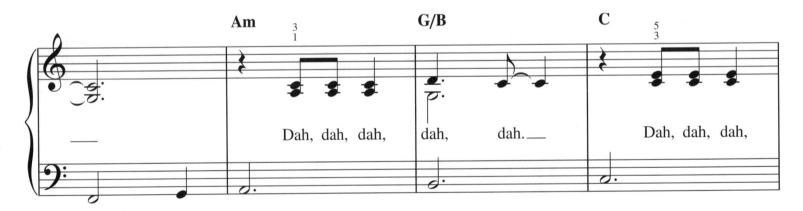

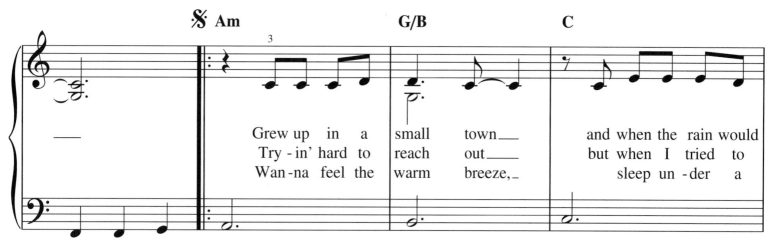

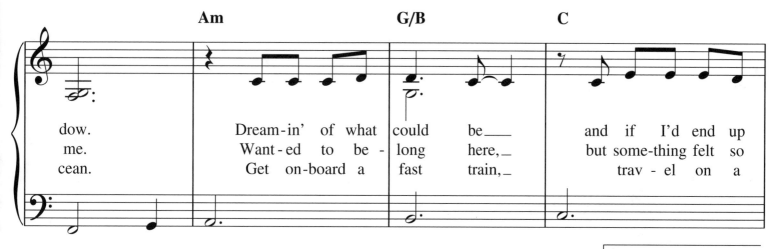

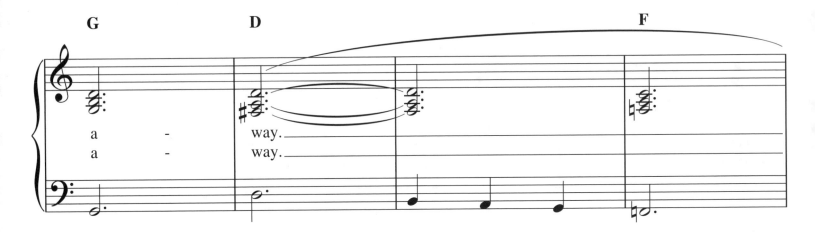

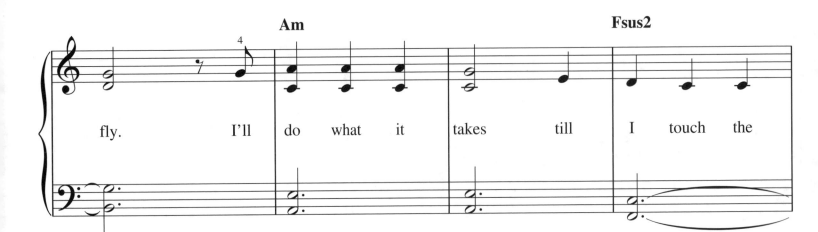

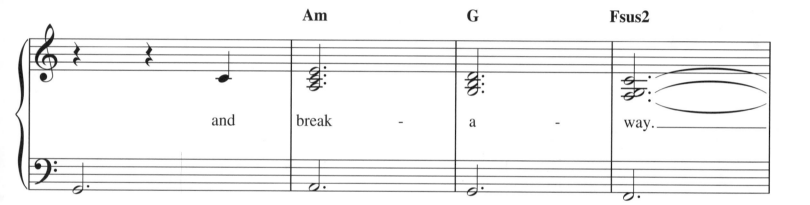

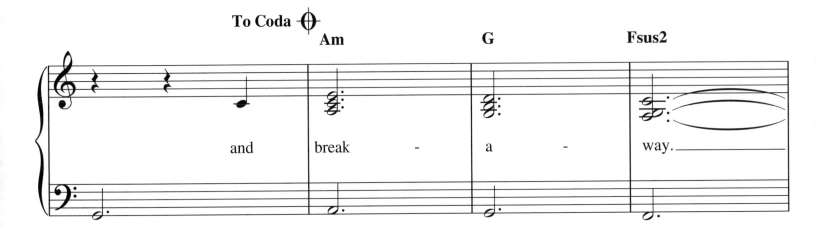

D.S. al Coda

CODA

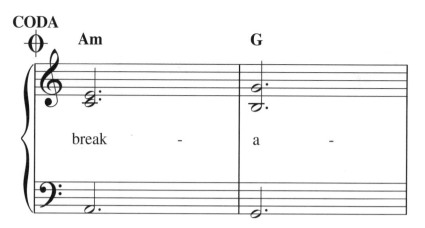

Am   **G**

break - a -

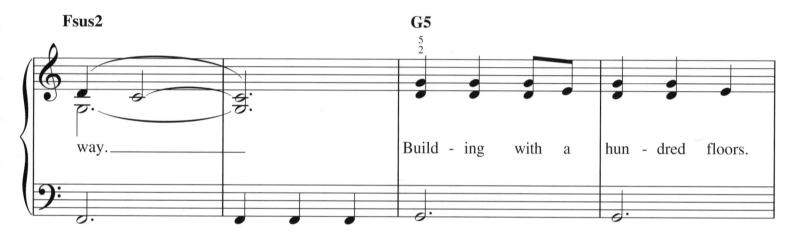

Fsus2   **G5**

way._____ Build - ing with a hun - dred floors.

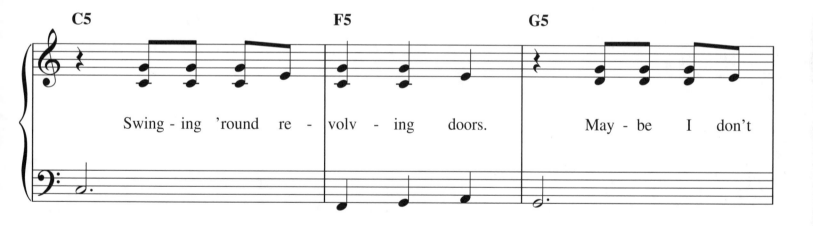

C5   **F5**   **G5**

Swing - ing 'round re - volv - ing doors. May - be I don't

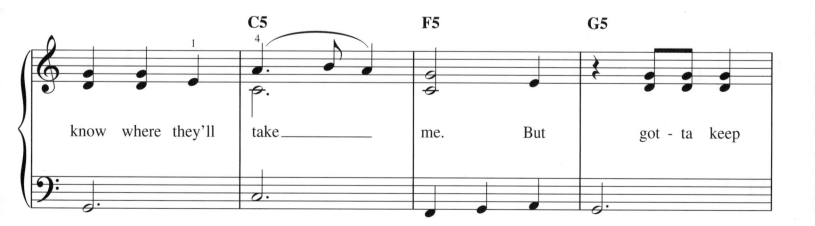

C5   **F5**   **G5**

know where they'll take_____ me. But got - ta keep

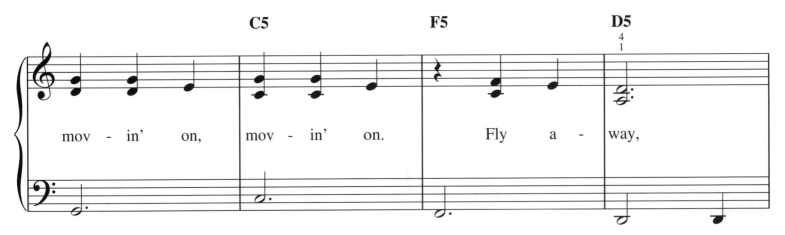

C5   **F5**   **D5**

mov - in' on,   mov - in' on.   Fly   a - way,

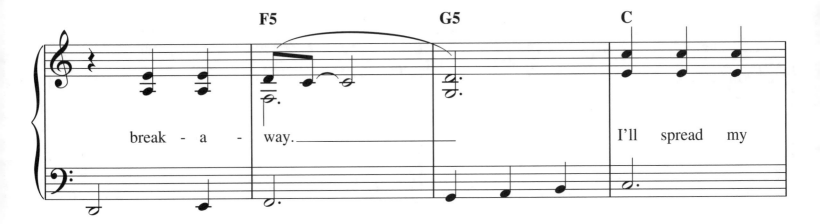

F5   **G5**   **C**

break - a - way. _____   I'll spread my

G   **Am**

wings and I'll   learn how to   fly.   Though it's not

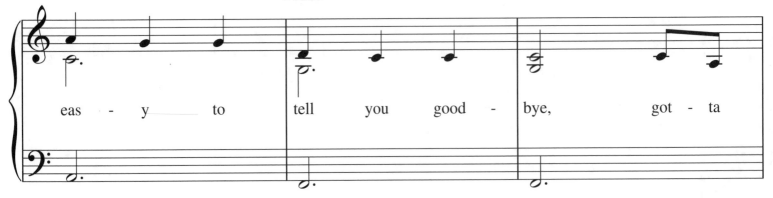

Fsus2

eas - y to   tell you good - bye,   got - ta

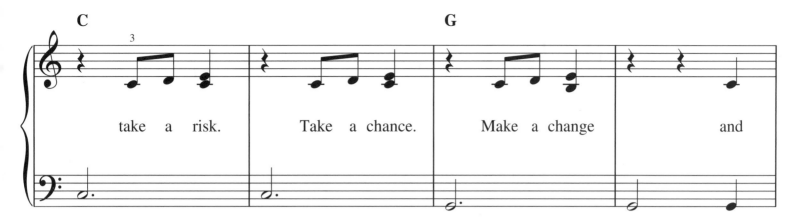

take a risk.　　Take a chance.　　Make a change　　and

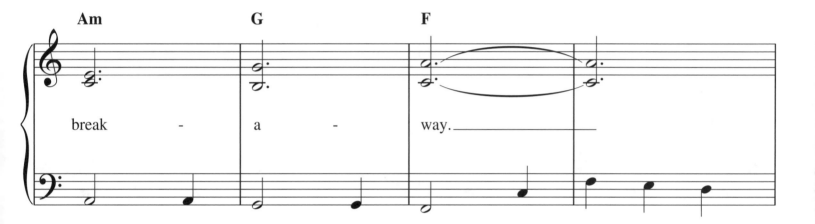

break　-　a　-　way.＿＿＿

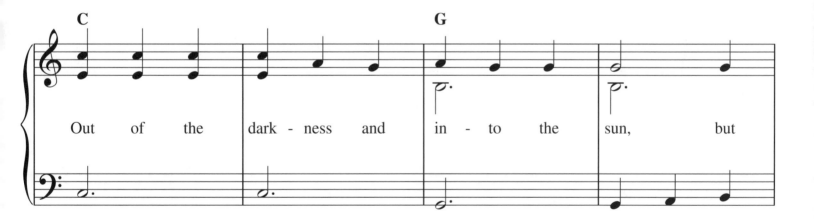

Out　of　the　dark - ness　and　in - to　the　sun,　but

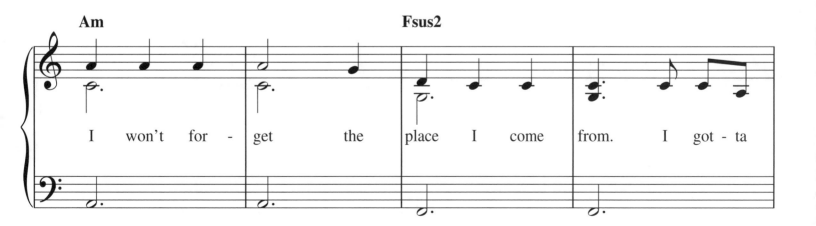

I　won't　for - get　the　place　I　come　from.　I　got - ta

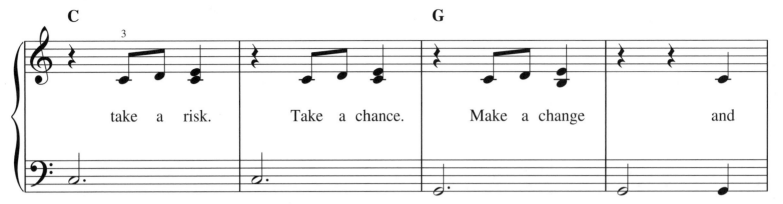

take a risk. Take a chance. Make a change and

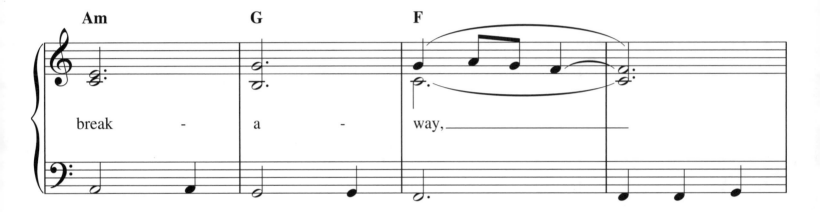

break - a - way,

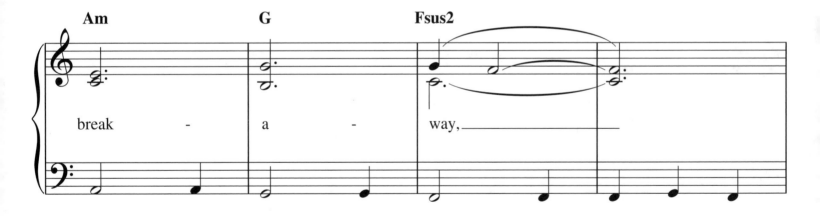

break - a - way,

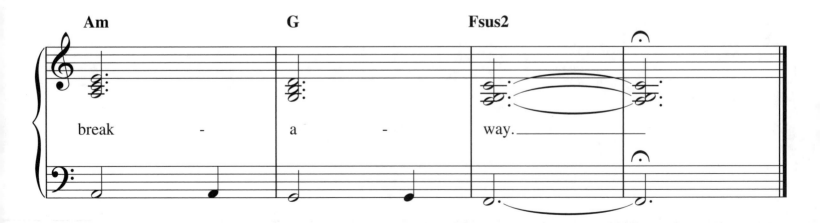

break - a - way.

BLESS THE BROKEN ROAD

Words and Music by MARCUS HUMMON,
BOBBY BOYD and JEFF HANNA

Moderately, with a half-time feel

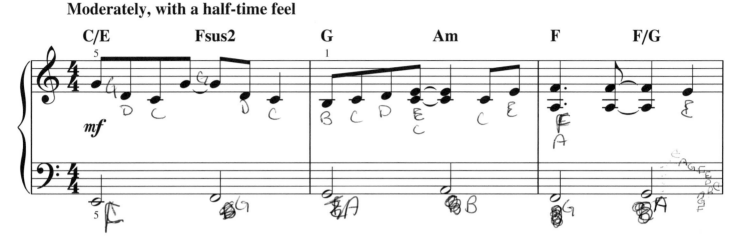

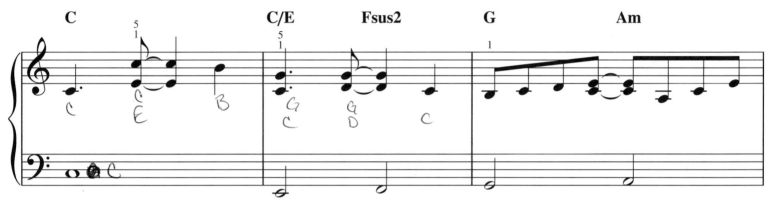

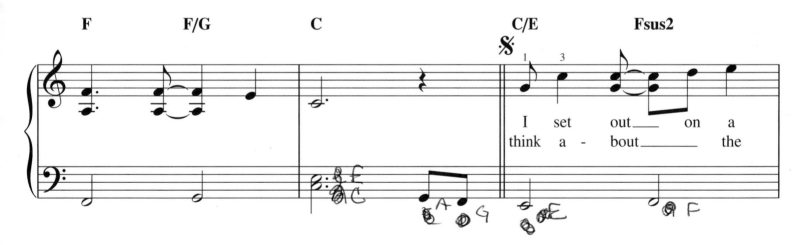

I set out___ on a
think a - bout_____ the

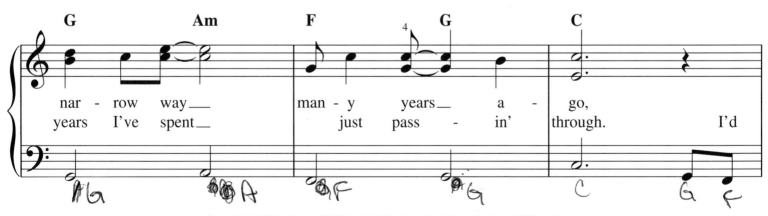

nar - row way___ man - y years___ a - go,
years I've spent___ just pass - in' through. I'd

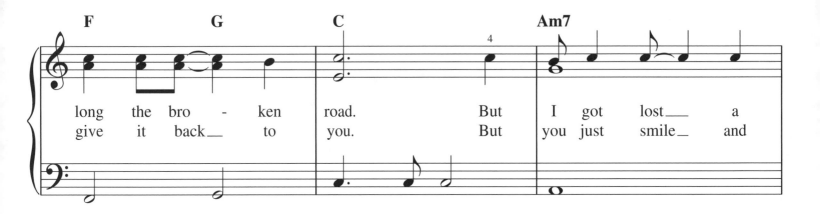

hop - ing   I_____ would   find____ true   love   a -
like   to   have____ the   time____ I   lost   and

long   the   bro - ken   road.   But   I   got   lost____ a
give   it   back____ to   you.   But   you   just   smile____ and

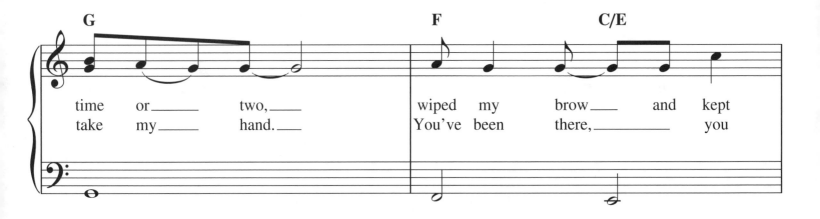

time   or_____ two,____   wiped   my   brow____ and   kept
take   my____ hand.____   You've   been   there,_____ you

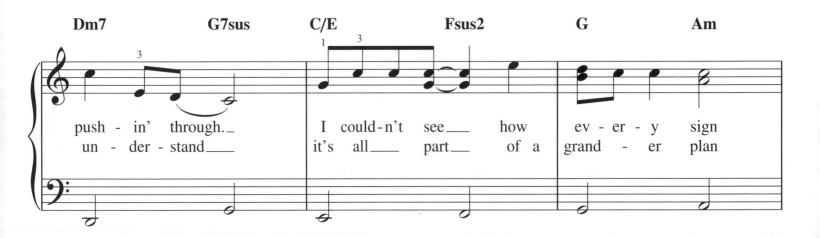

push - in'   through.____   I   could-n't   see____ how   ev - er - y   sign
un - der - stand____   it's   all____ part____ of   a   grand - er   plan

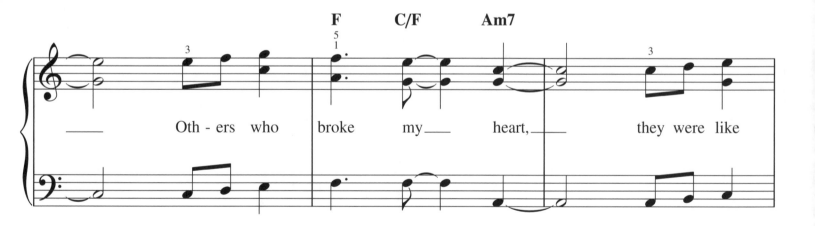

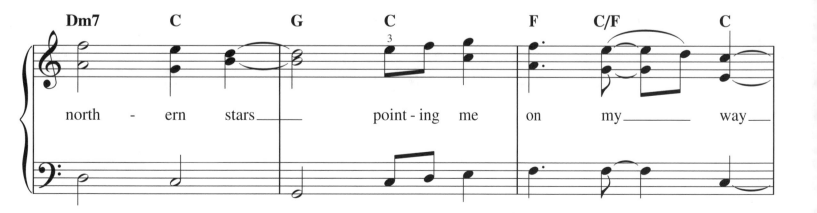

in - to your lov - ing arms. This much I

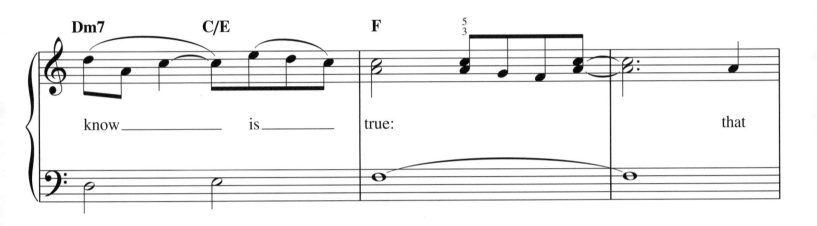

know is true: that

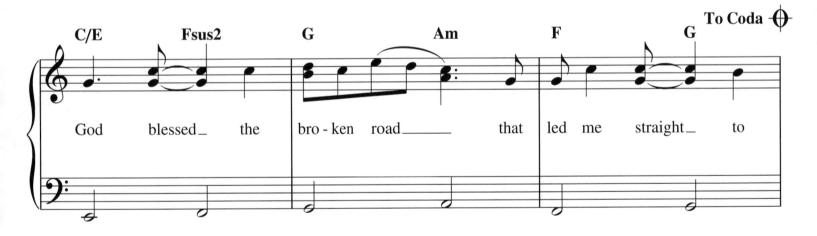

God blessed the bro - ken road that led me straight to

you.

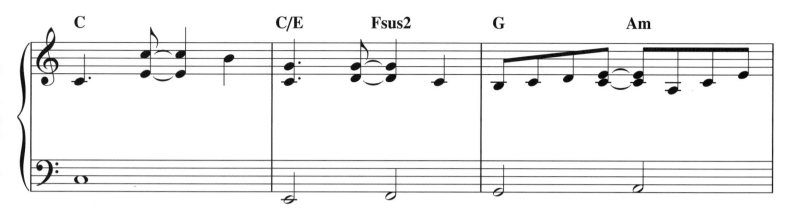

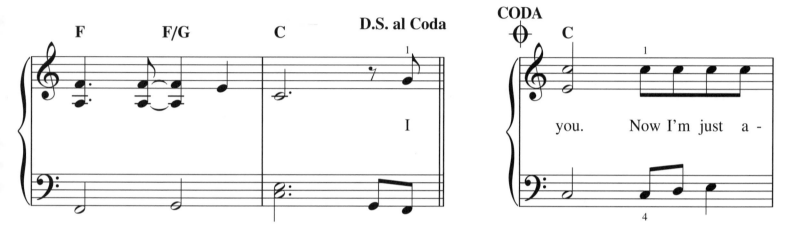

roll - in'___ home___ in - to my lov - er's___ arms.

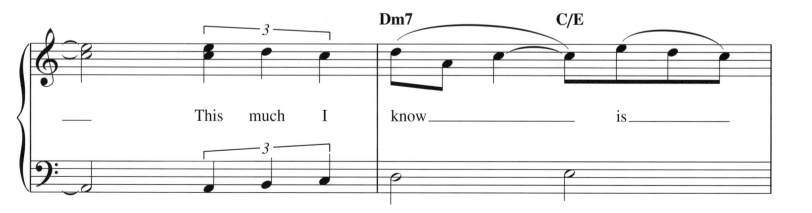

___ This much I know_____ is_____

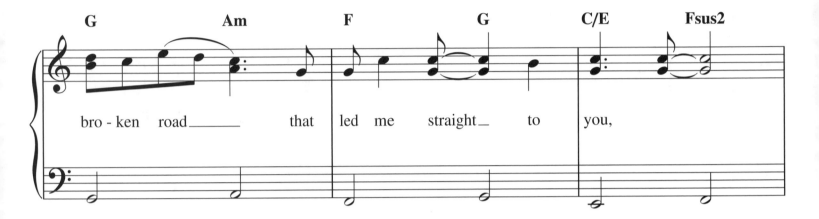

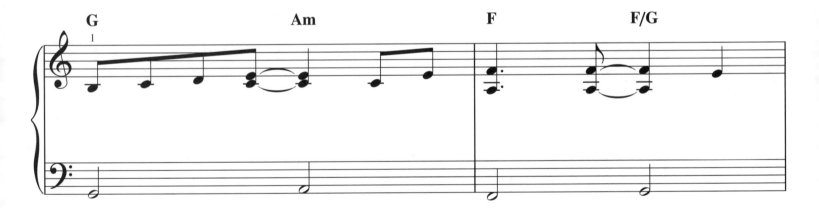

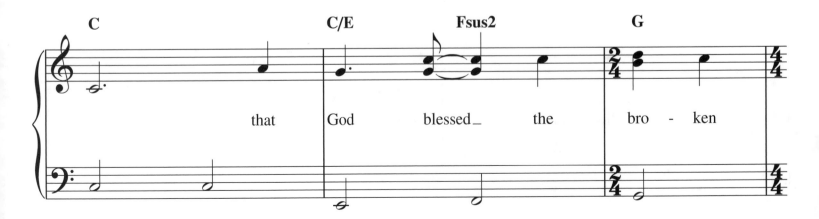

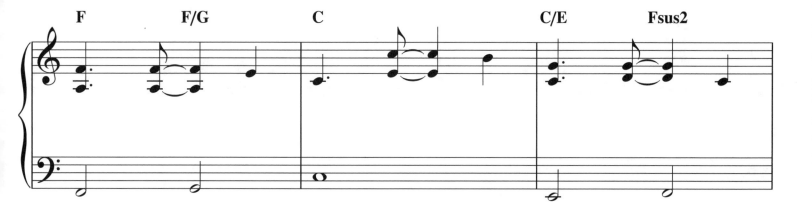

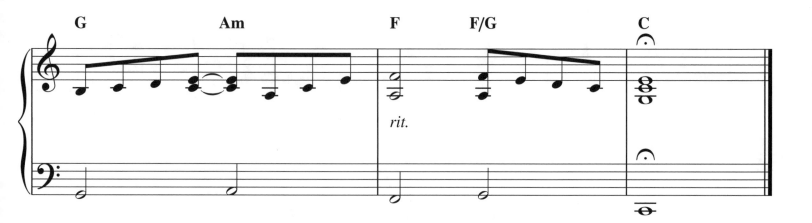

GIVE A LITTLE BIT

Words and Music by RICK DAVIES
and ROGER HODGSON

Moderate Rock

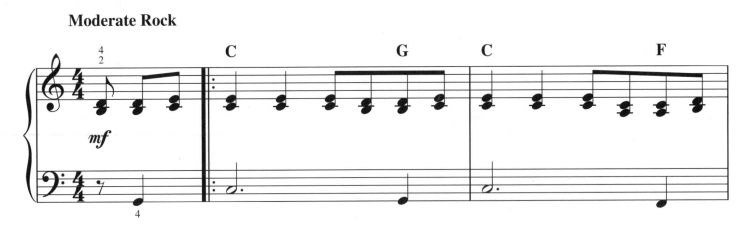

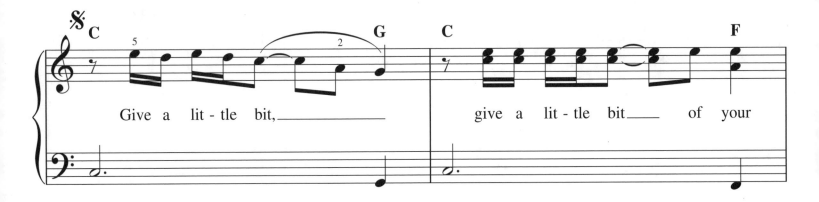

Give a lit-tle bit,_____ give a lit-tle bit_____ of your

love to me.   I'll give a lit-tle bit,_____

I'll give a lit-tle bit___ of my { love to you. / life for you.

There's so much___ that we need to share,___ so
Now the time___ that we need to share,___ so

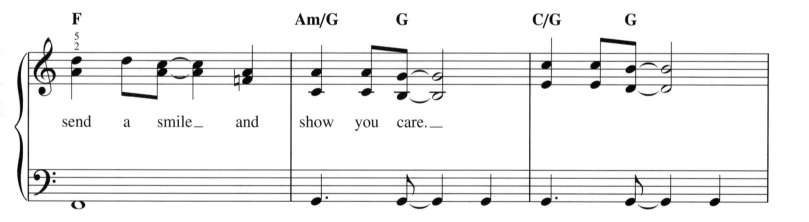

send a smile_ and show you care._

I'll give a lit-tle bit,_____ I'll give a lit-tle bit___ of my

life for you.

So give a lit-tle bit,_____

oh, give a lit-tle bit____ of your time to me.

See the man____ with the lone - ly eyes?____ Oh,

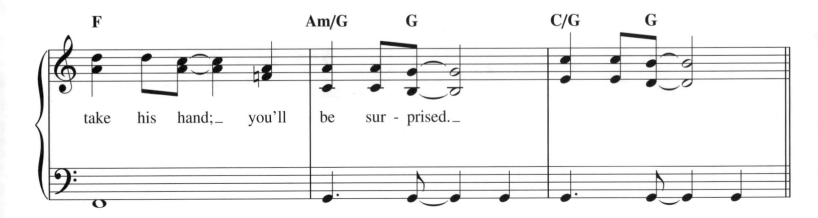

take his hand;__ you'll be sur - prised.__

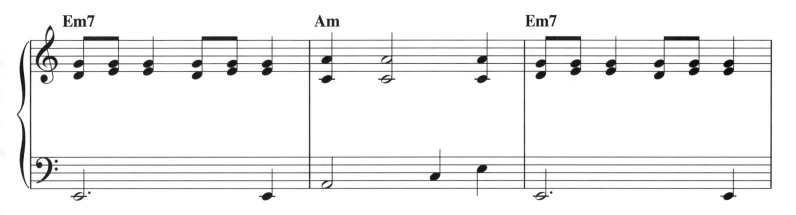

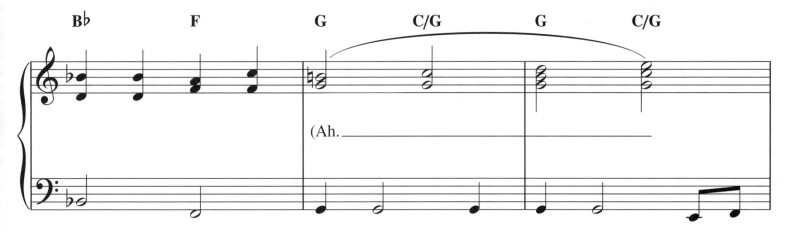

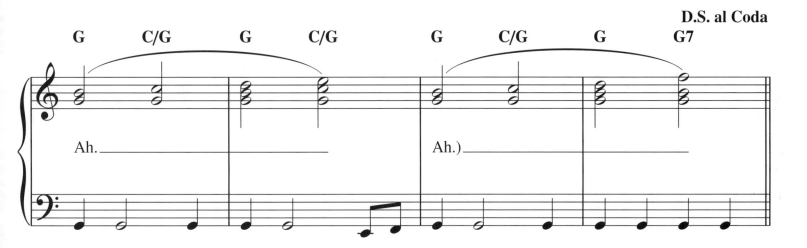

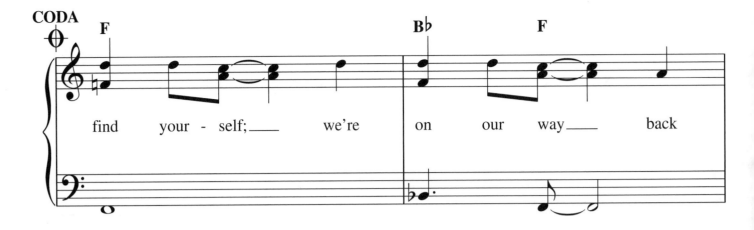

find   your - self;____   we're   on   our   way____   back

home.   Oh,   go - in'   home.

Don't you need, don't you need   to   feel   at   home?

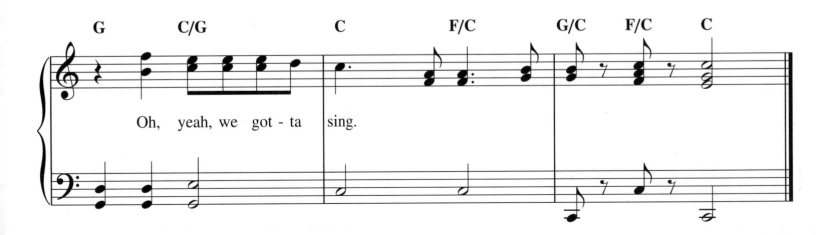

Oh,   yeah, we got - ta   sing.

HOME

Words and Music by AMY FOSTER-GILLIES,
MICHAEL BUBLÉ and ALAN CHANG

Moderately slow

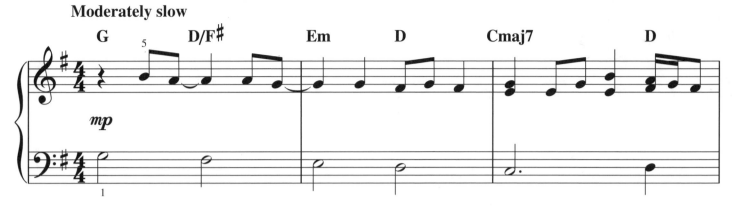

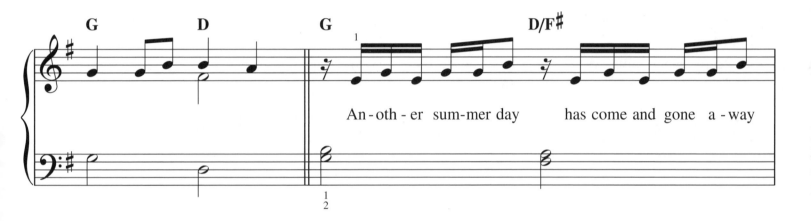

An-oth-er sum-mer day has come and gone a-way

in Par-is and Rome, but I wan-na go home.

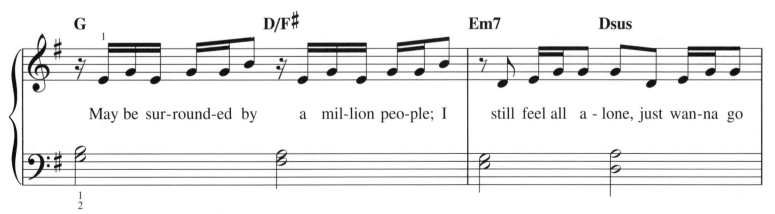

May be sur-round-ed by a mil-lion peo-ple; I   still feel all a-lone, just wan-na go

home.   Oh, I miss you, you know.   I've been

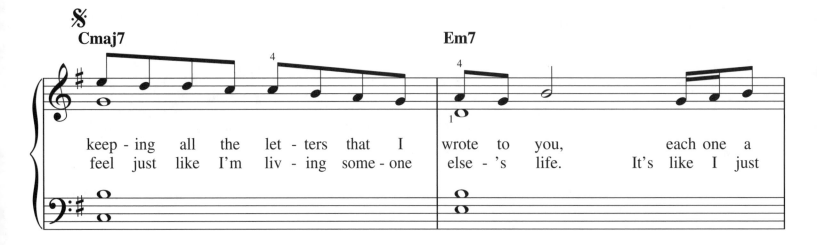

keep - ing all the let - ters that I   wrote to you,   each one a
feel just like I'm liv - ing some - one else - 's life.   It's like I just

line or two,   "I'm fine, ba - by, how are you?"   I would
stepped out - side when ev - 'ry-thing was go - ing right.   And I

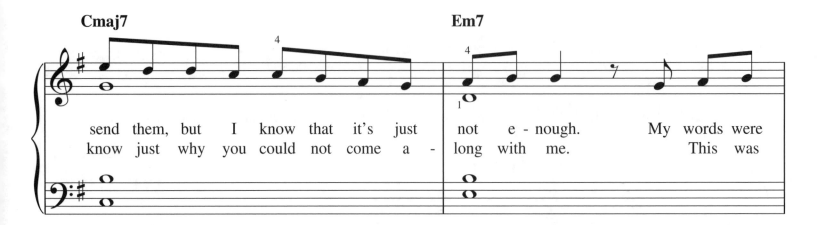

send them, but I know that it's just not e - nough.   My words were
know just why you could not come a -   long with me.   This was

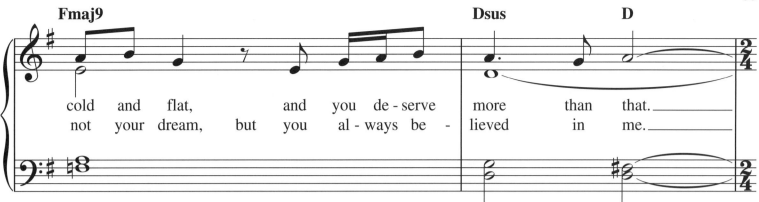

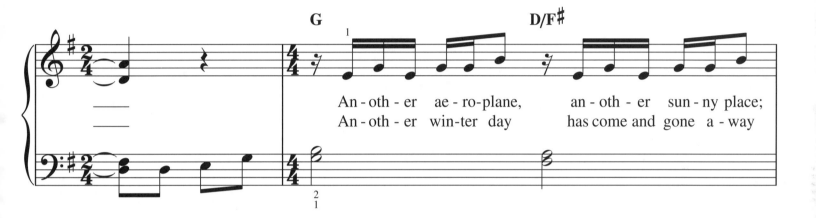

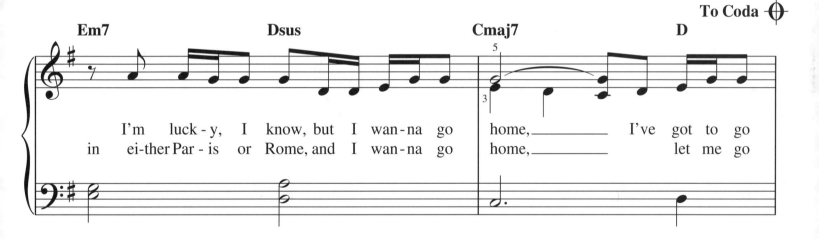

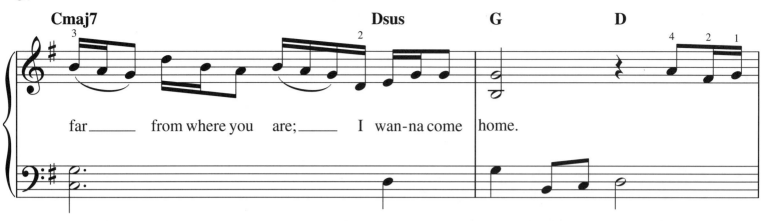

far_____ from where you are;_____ I wan-na come home.

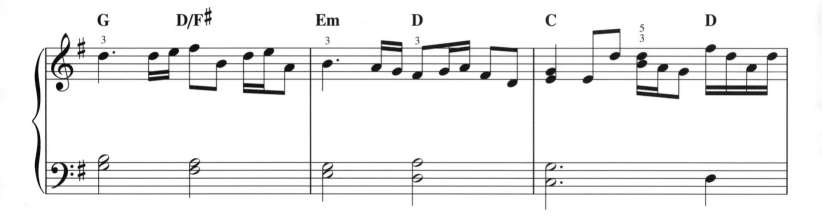

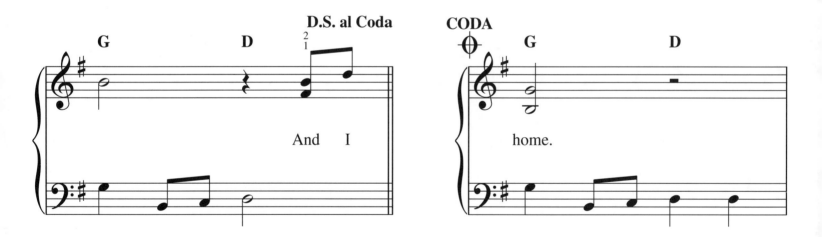

And I

home.

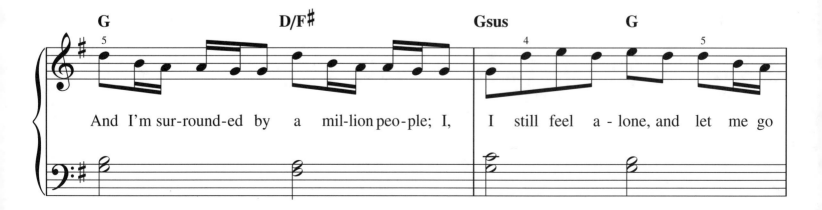

And I'm sur-round-ed by a mil-lion peo-ple; I, I still feel a - lone, and let me go

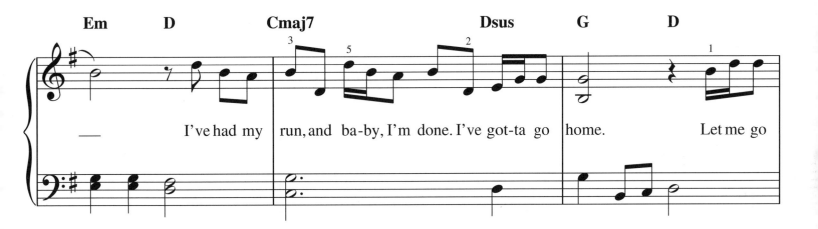

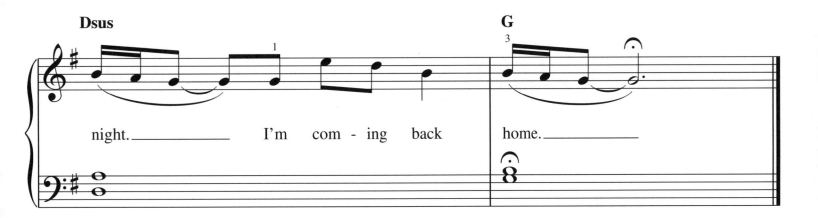

HEAVEN

Words and Music by HENRY GARZA,
JOEY GARZA and RINGO GARZA

Save_____ me from this pris - on.__

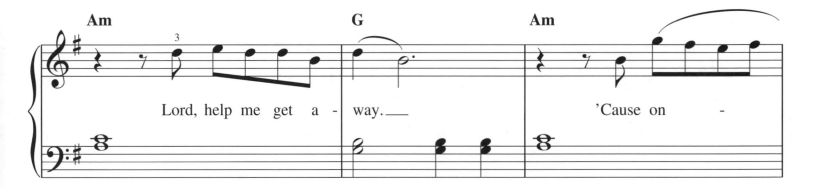

Lord, help me get a - way.__ 'Cause on -

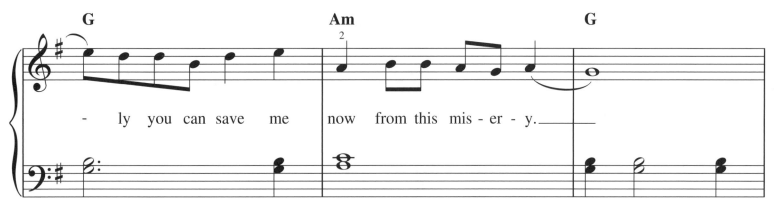

- ly you can save me now from this mis - er - y.

I've been lost in my own place and I'm get-tin' wea -

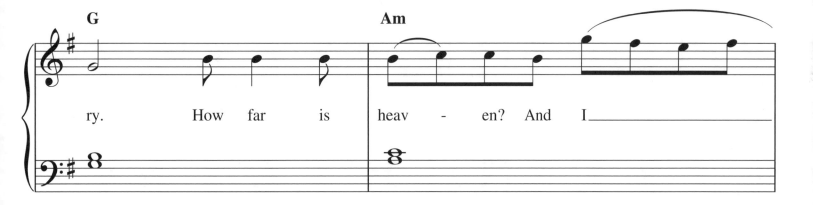

ry. How far is heav - en? And I

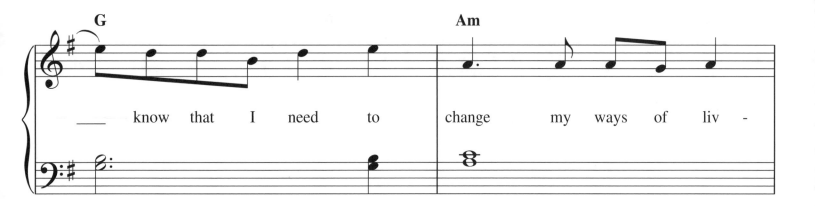

know that I need to change my ways of liv -

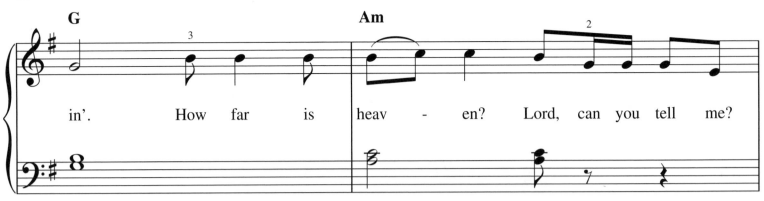

in'. How far is heav - en? Lord, can you tell me?

I've_____ been locked up way too
_____ know there's a bet - ter

long in this cra - zy world._____ How far is
place than this place I'm liv - in'._____ How far is

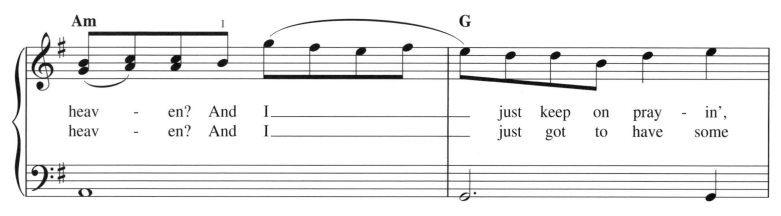

heav - en? And I_____ just keep on pray - in',
heav - en? And I_____ just got to have some

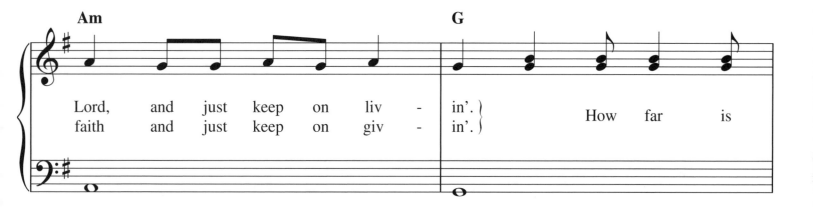

Lord, and just keep on liv - in'. }
faith and just keep on giv - in'. } How far is

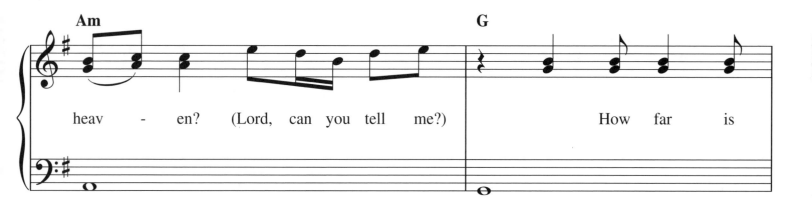

heav - en? (Lord, can you tell me?) How far is

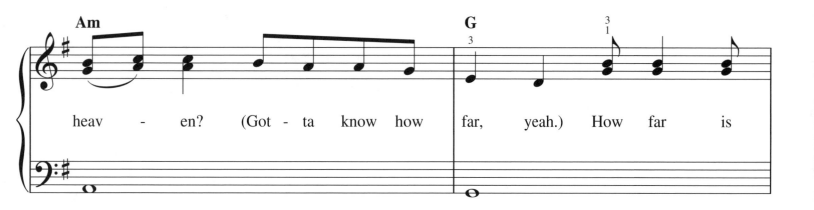

heav - en? (Got - ta know how far, yeah.) How far is

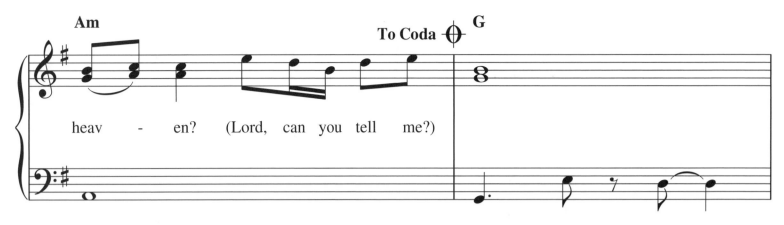

heav - en? (Lord, can you tell me?)

Tú que_es-tás en - tra-do_al cie - lo.___

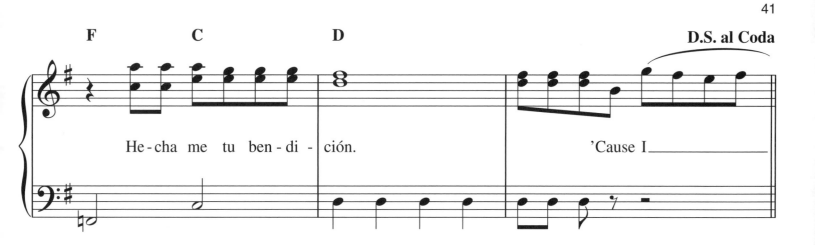

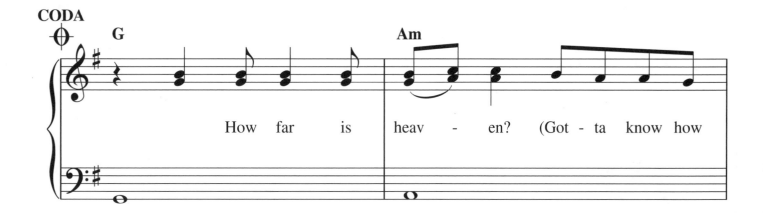

KARMA

Words and Music by KERRY BROTHERS, JR.,
ALICIA KEYS and TANEISHA SMITH

Moderately slow

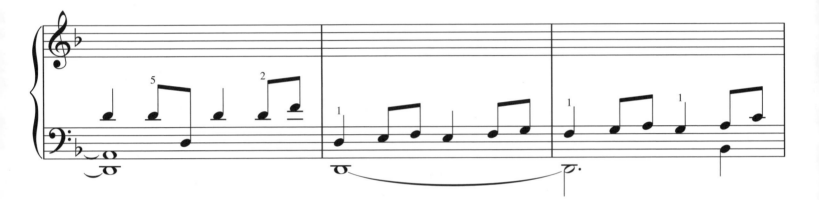

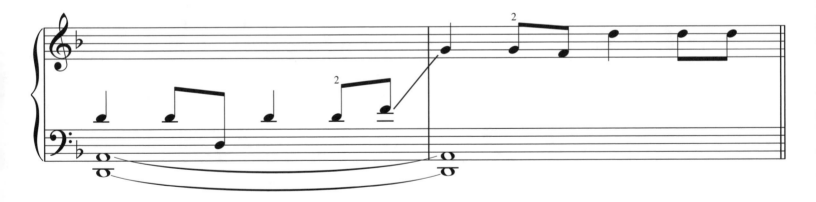

Weren't you the one that said that | you don't want me an - y - more,
And when you came home, you'd al - | ways have some sor - ry ex - cuse,

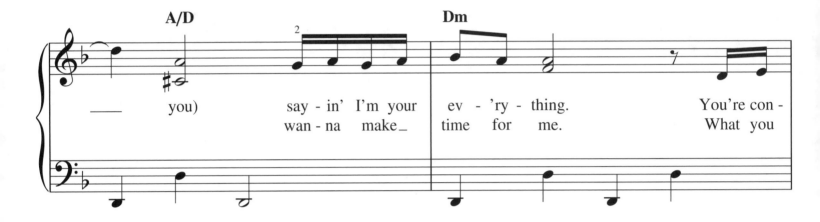

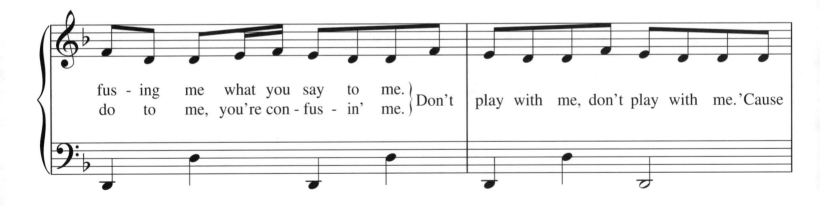

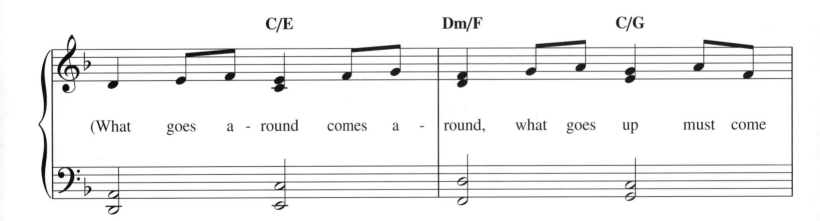

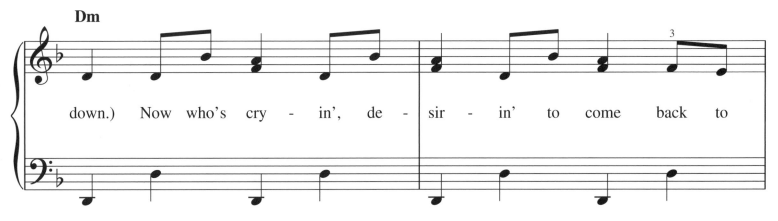

Dm

down.) Now who's cry - in', de - sir - in' to come back to

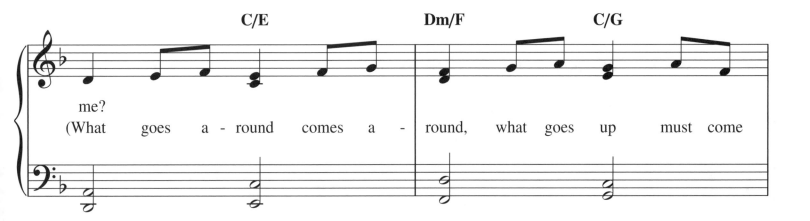

C/E   **Dm/F**   **C/G**

me?
(What goes a - round comes a - round, what goes up must come

Dm

down.) Now who's cry - in', de - sir - in' to come back?

1.
N.C.

I re-mem-ber when I was sit-tin' home a-lone, wait-in' for you 'til three o'-clock in the morn.

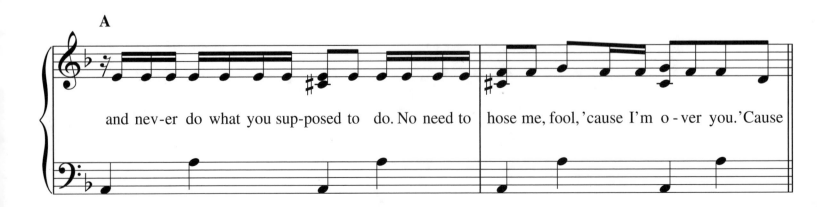

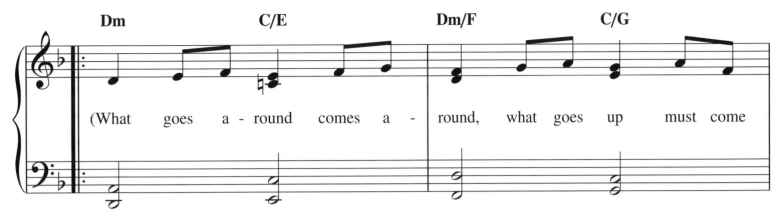

(What goes a-round comes a-round, what goes up must come

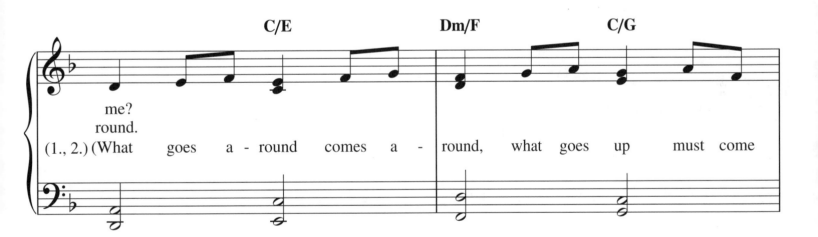

down.)
Now who's cry-in', de-sir-in' to come back to
It's called kar-ma, ba-by, and it goes_____ a-

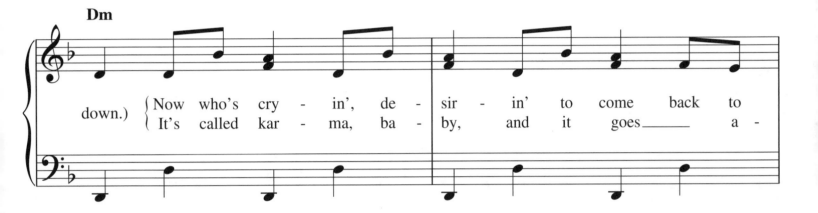

me?
round.
(1., 2.) (What goes a-round comes a-round, what goes up must come

down.) Got-ta stop try-in'   to come back to me._____

48

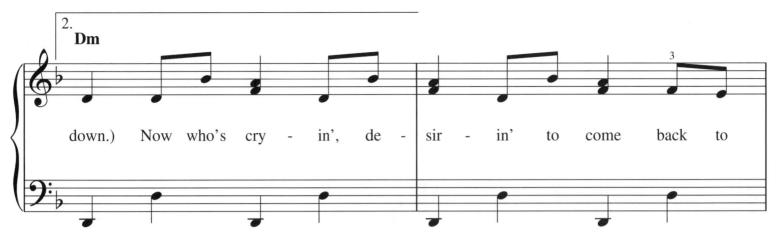

down.) Now who's cry - in', de - sir - in' to come back to

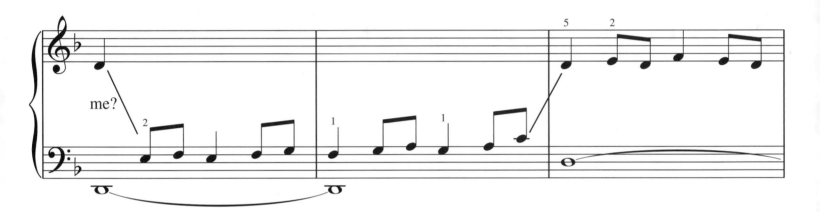

me?

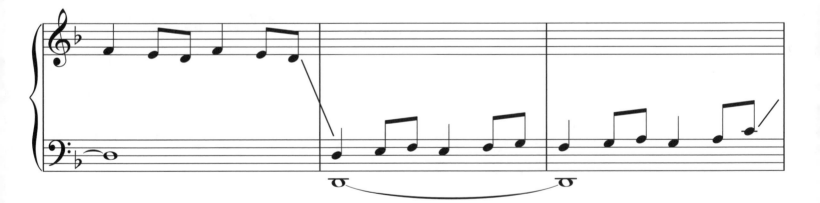

LET ME GO

Words and Music by BRAD ARNOLD,
ROBERT HARRELL, CHRISTOPHER HENDERSON
and MATTHEW ROBERTS

Moderate Rock

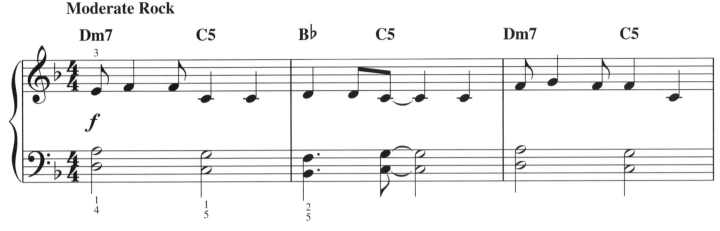

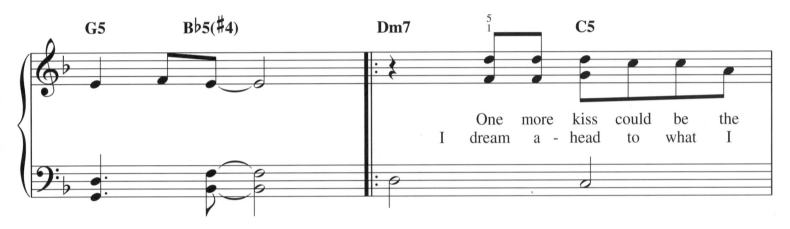

One more kiss could be the best thing. ___
I dream a - head to what I hope for. ___

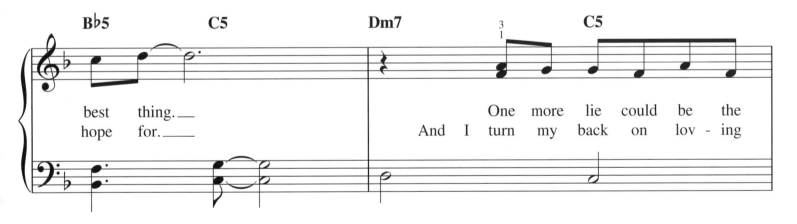

One more lie could be the worst.
And I turn my back on lov - ing you.

And all these thoughts are nev - er
How can this love be a

rest - ing.____
good thing?__

And you're not some - thing I de -
And I know what I'm go - ing

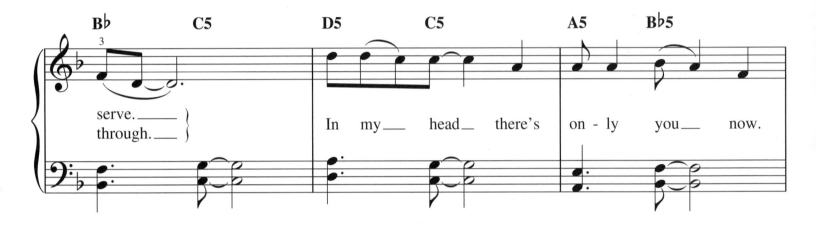

serve.____
through.__

In my__ head__ there's on - ly you__ now.

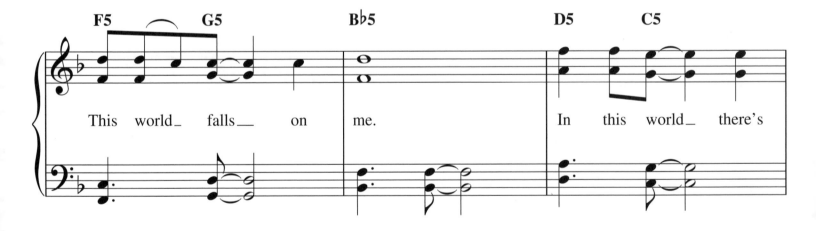

This world_ falls__ on me.

In this world_ there's

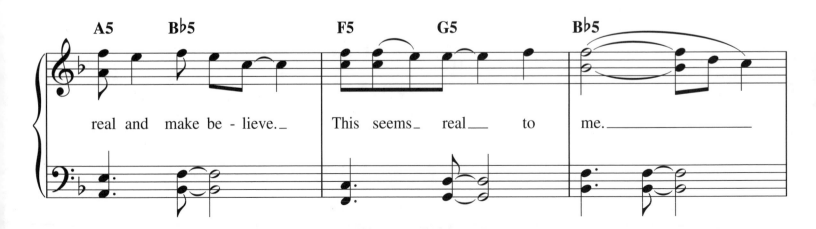

real and make be - lieve.__

This seems_ real__ to me._____

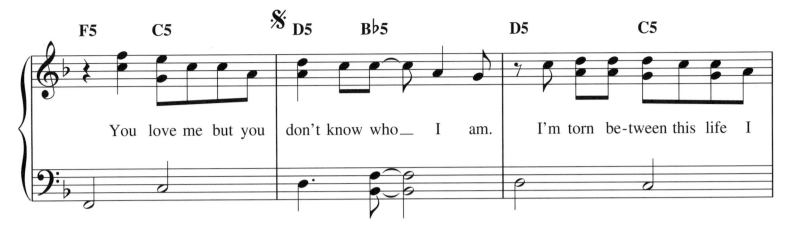

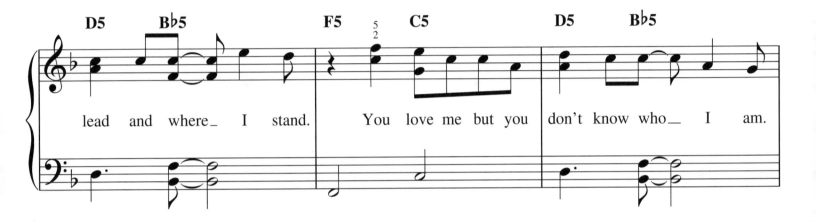

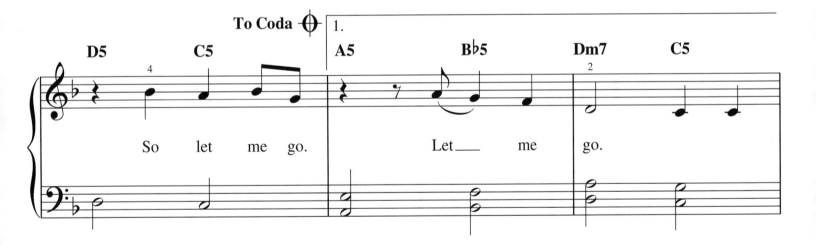

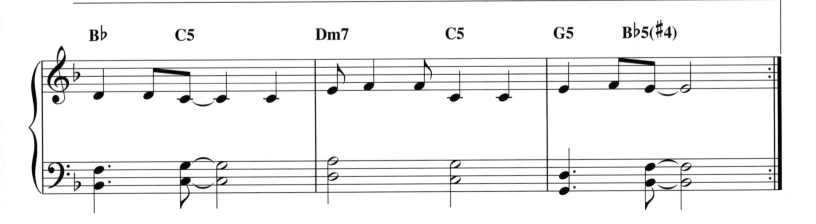

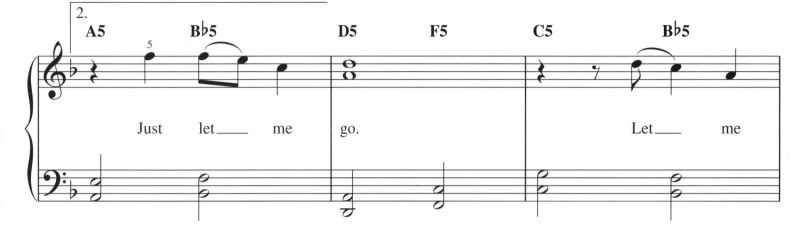

Just let___ me go. Let___ me

go. And no mat - ter how hard I try, I

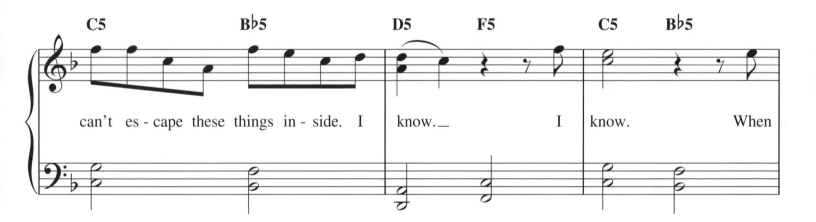

can't es - cape these things in - side. I know.___ I know. When

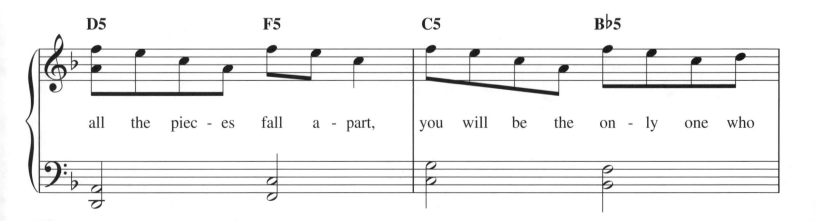

all the piec - es fall a - part, you will be the on - ly one who

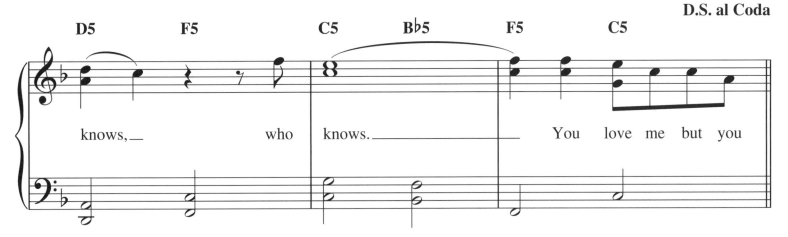

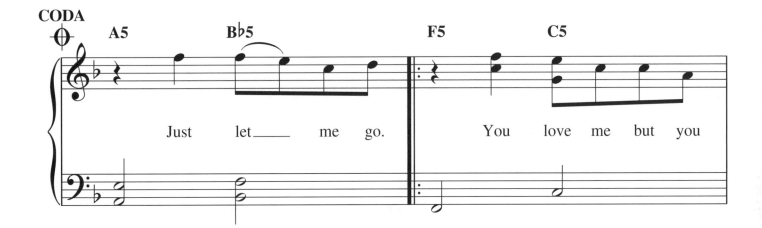

LIVE LIKE YOU WERE DYING

Words and Music by CRAIG WISEMAN
and TIM J. NICHOLS

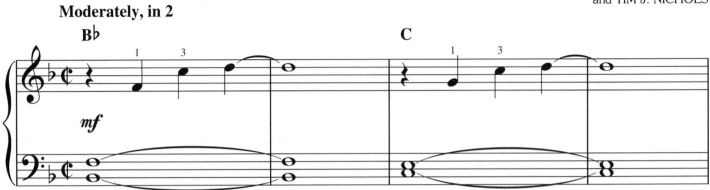

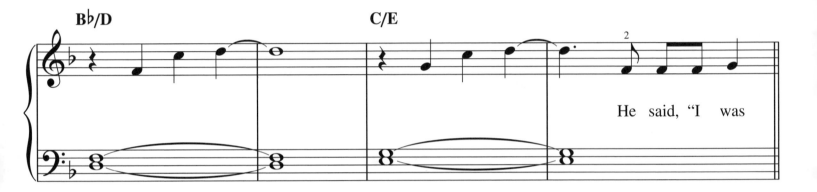

He said, "I was

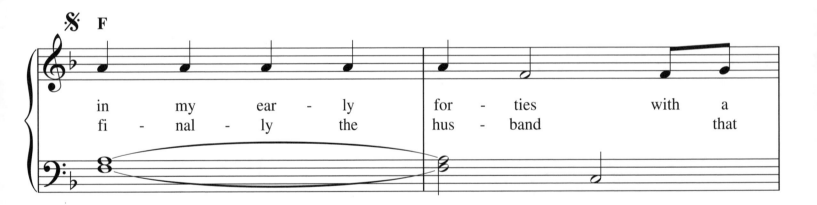

in my ear - ly
fi - nal - ly the

for - ties
hus - band

with a
that

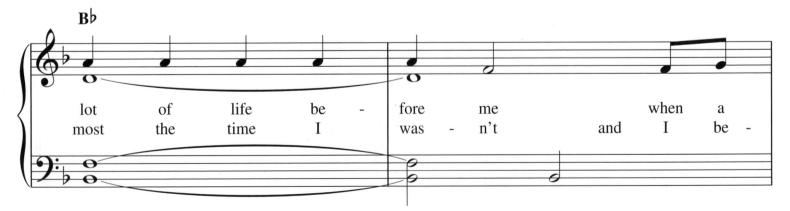

lot of life be - fore me when a
most the life time I was - n't and I be -

mo - ment came that stopped me on a dime.___
came a friend a friend would like to have.___

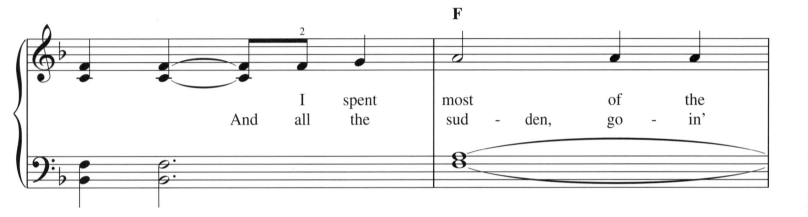

I spent most of the
And all the sud - den, go - in'

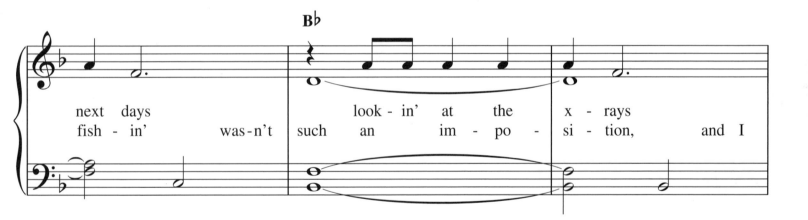

next days look - in' at the x - rays
fish - in' was-n't such an im - po - si - tion, and I

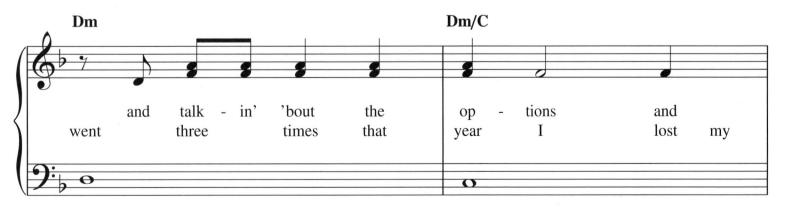

and talk - in' 'bout the op - tions and
went three times that year I lost my

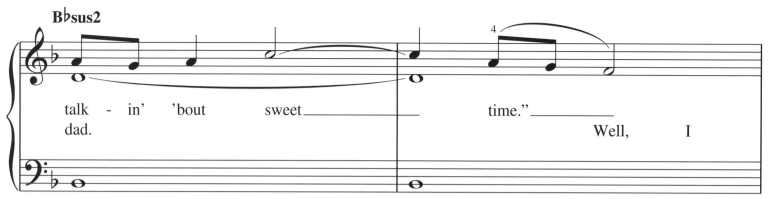

B♭sus2

talk - in' 'bout sweet_____ time."_____
dad.   Well, I

Dm

    I   asked   him,   when it sank in_____ that
fi - n'lly read the   Good Book and_____ I

F+/C♯

this might real - ly   be the real end, how's it
took a good long   hard look at what I'd

F/C

hit you   when you   get that kind of news?____
do if   when I could   do it all a - gain.____

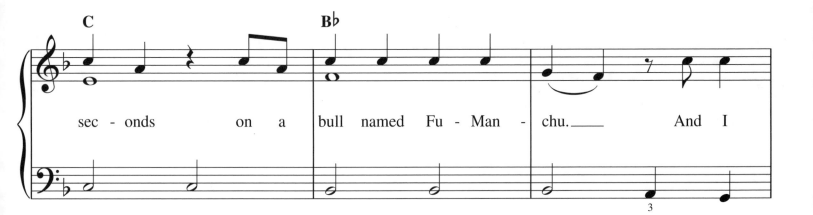

58

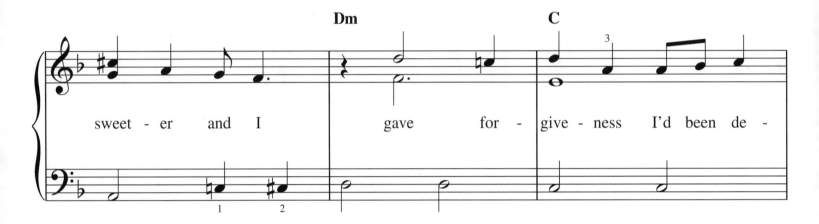

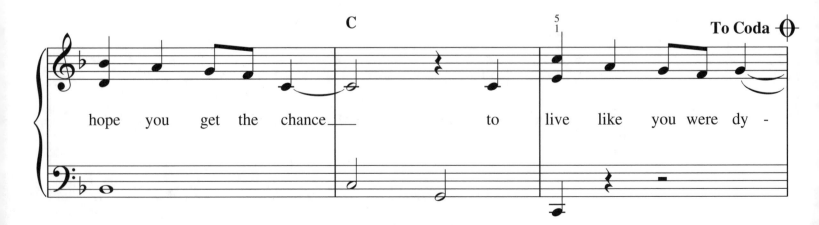

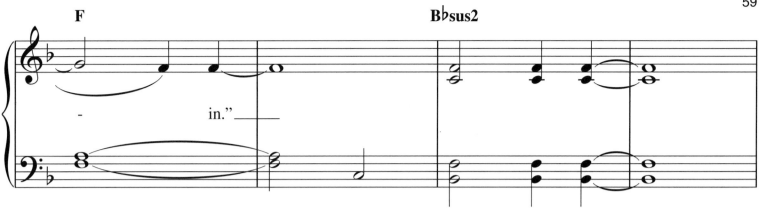

-in."

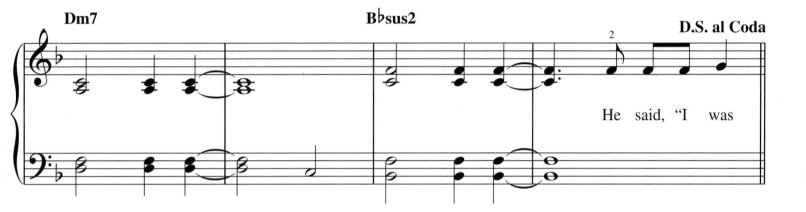

He said, "I was

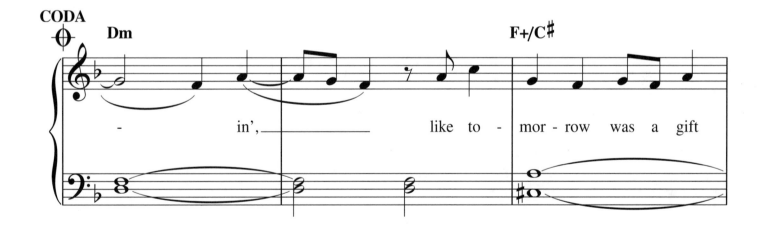

-in', like to - mor - row was a gift

and you got e - ter - ni - ty to think a - bout what you'd

do with it." What could you do with it?

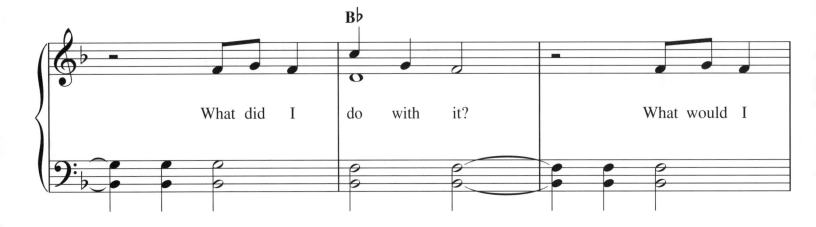

What did I do with it? What would I

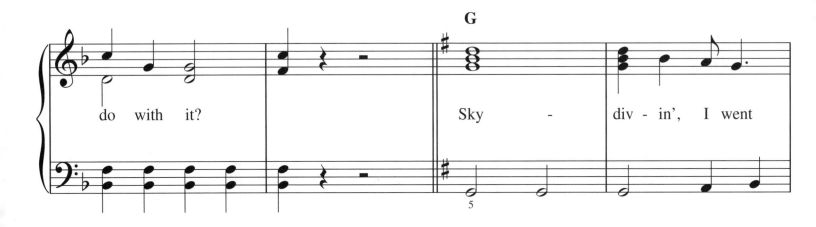

do with it? Sky - div - in', I went

Rock - y Moun - tain climb - in', I went two point sev - en

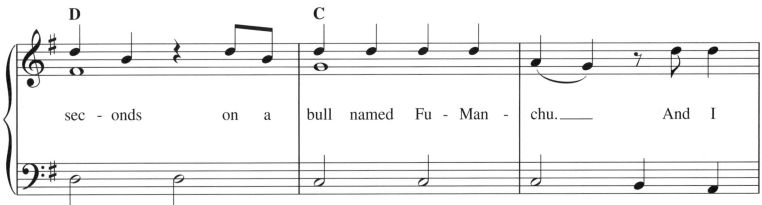

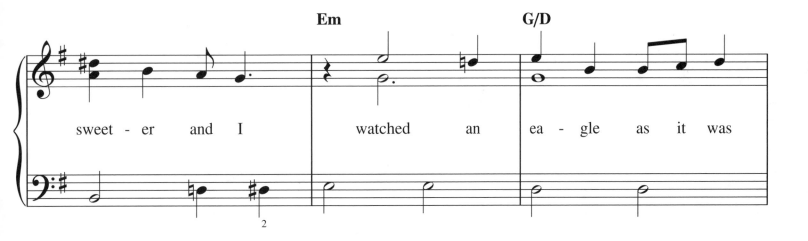

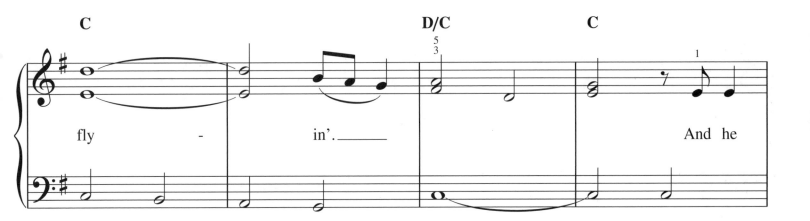

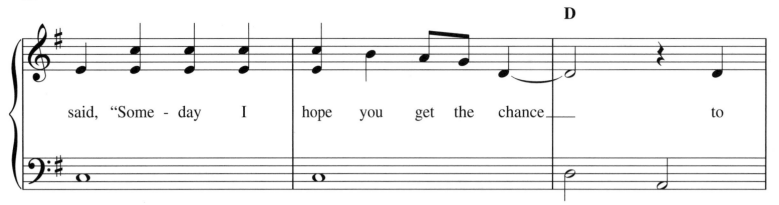

said, "Some - day I hope you get the chance_____ to

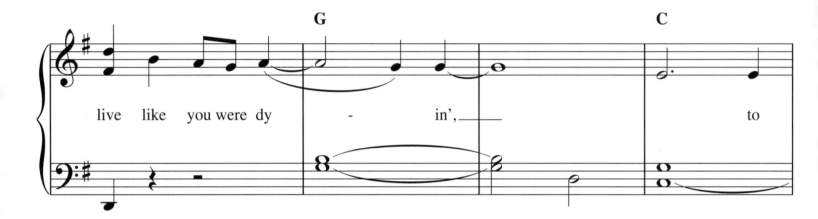

live like you were dy - in',_____ to

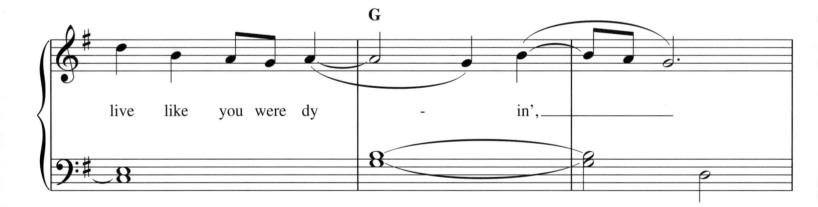

live like you were dy - in',_____

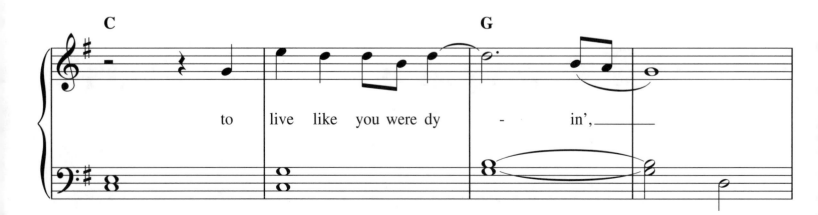

to live like you were dy - in',_____

to live like you were dy - in',

to live like you were dy -

- -

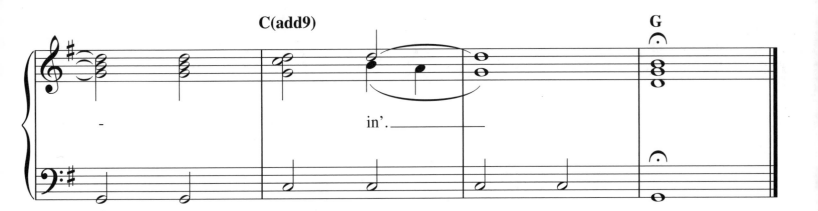

- in'.

SHE WILL BE LOVED

Words and Music by ADAM LEVINE
and JAMES VALENTINE

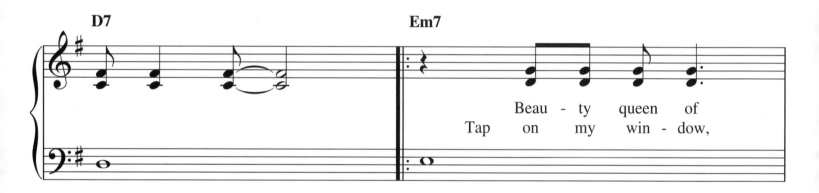

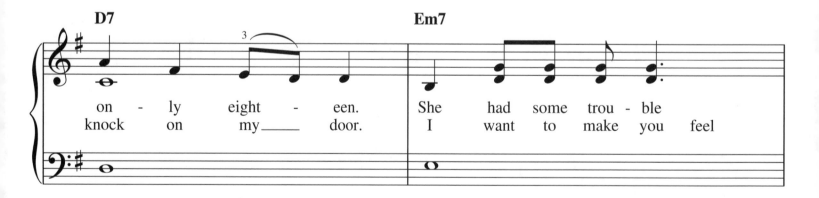

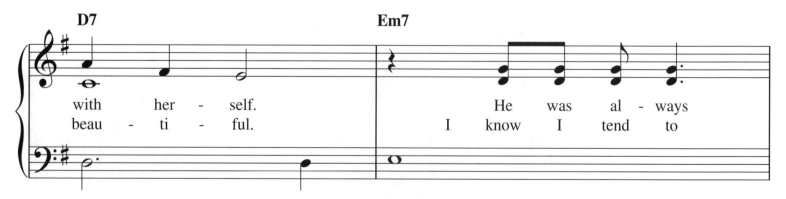

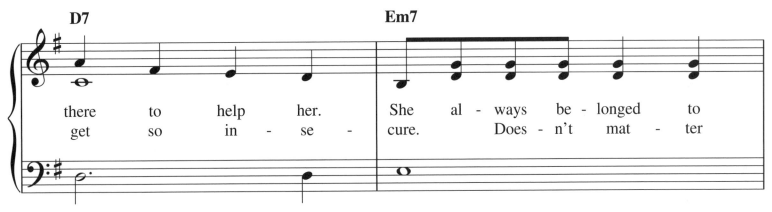

there to help her. She al - ways be - longed to
get so in - se - cure. Does - n't mat - ter

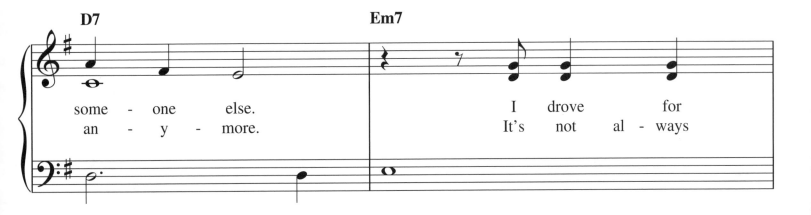

some - one else. I drove for
an - y - more. It's not al - ways

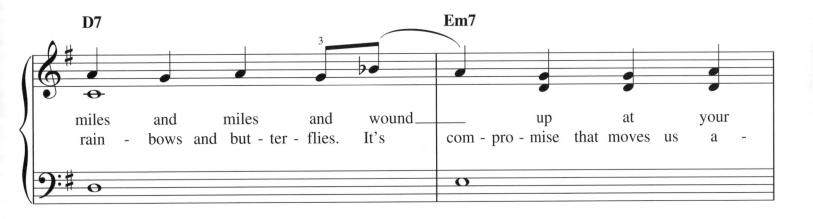

miles and miles and wound___ up at your
rain - bows and but - ter - flies. It's com - pro - mise that moves us a -

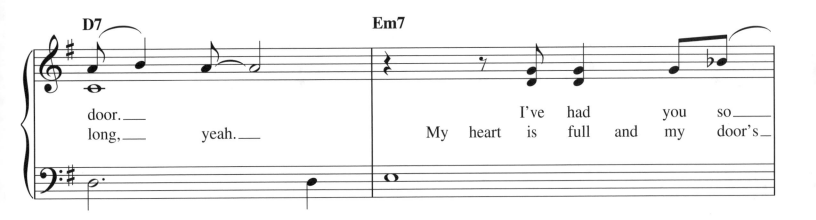

door.___ I've had you so___
long,___ yeah.___ My heart is full and my door's___

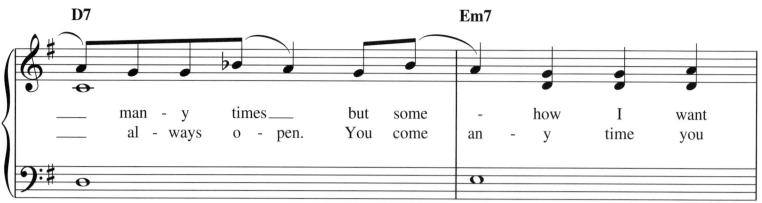

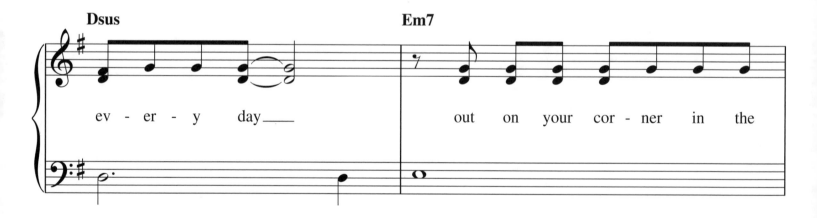

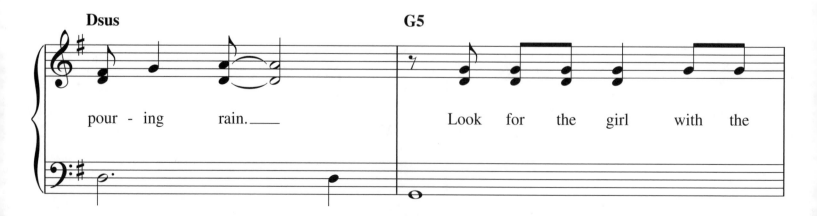

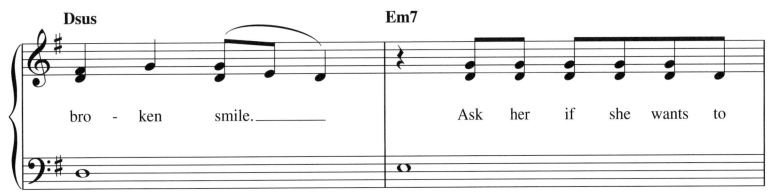

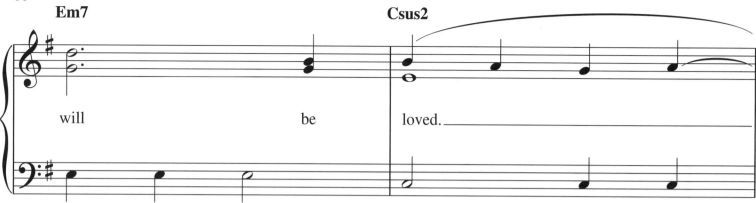

will   be   loved.

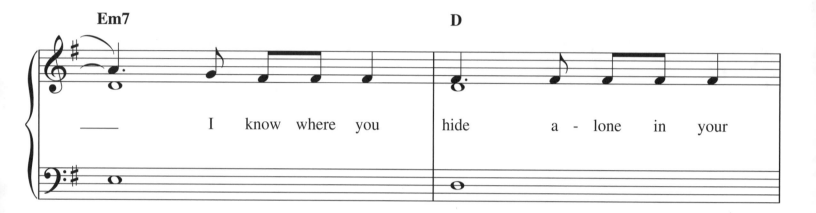

_____   I   know   where   you   hide   a - lone   in   your

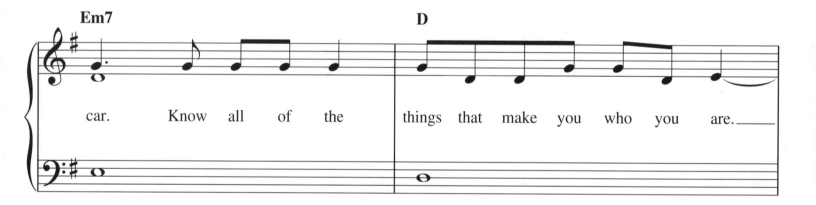

car.   Know   all   of   the   things   that   make   you   who   you   are._____

_____   I   know   that   good - bye   means   noth - ing   at

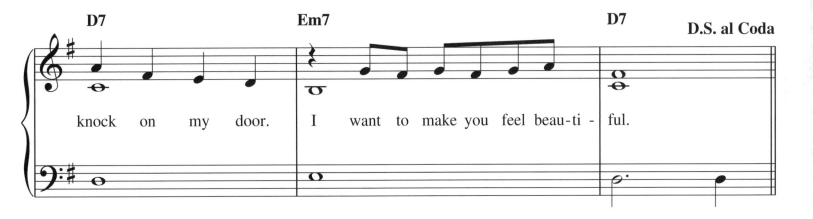

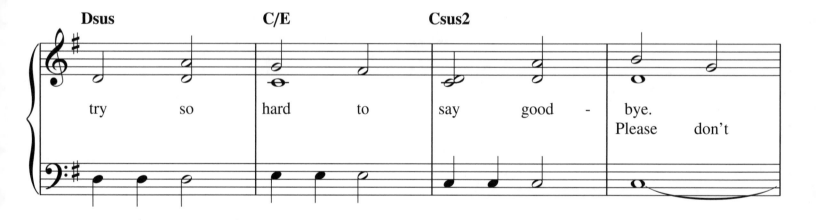

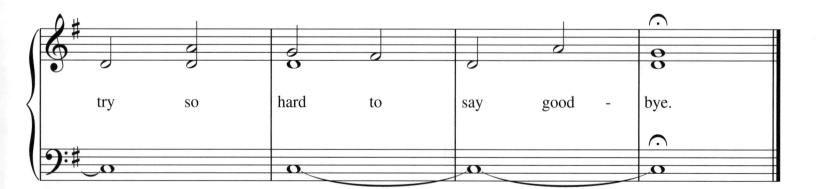

LONELY NO MORE

Words and Music by
ROB THOMAS

Moderate groove

Now it seems to me that you

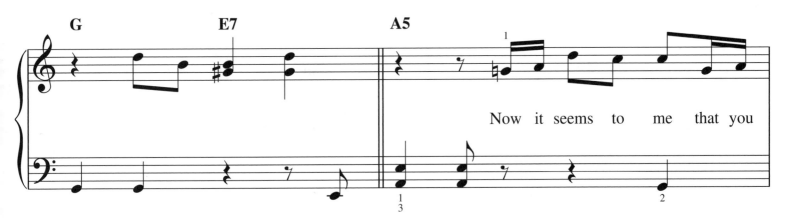

know just what to say. But words are on-ly

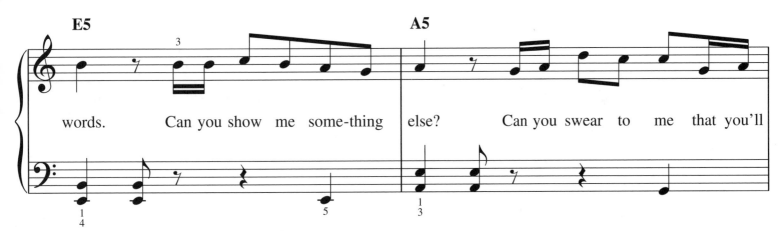

words. Can you show me some-thing else? Can you swear to me that you'll

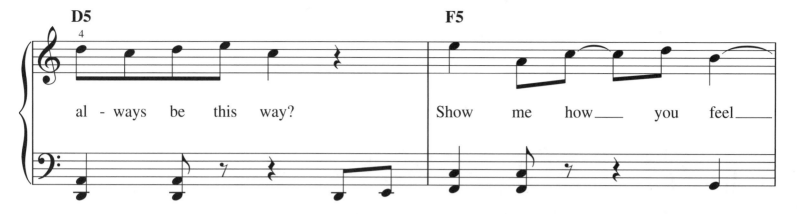

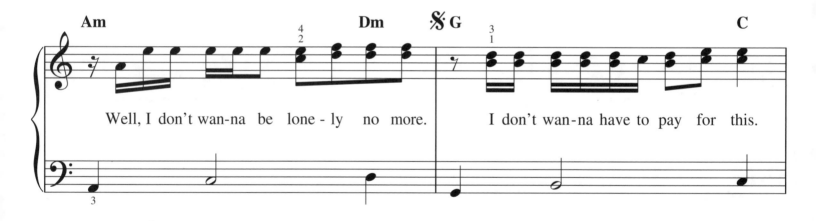

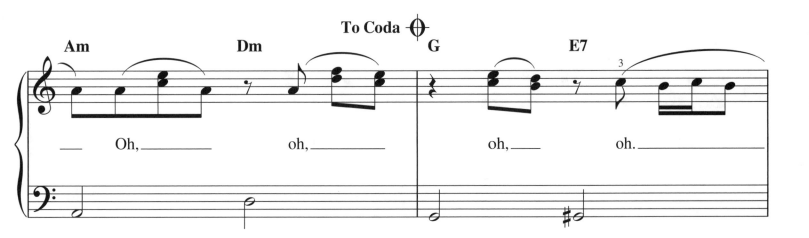

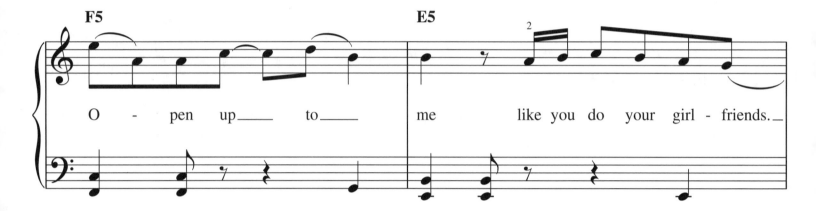

75

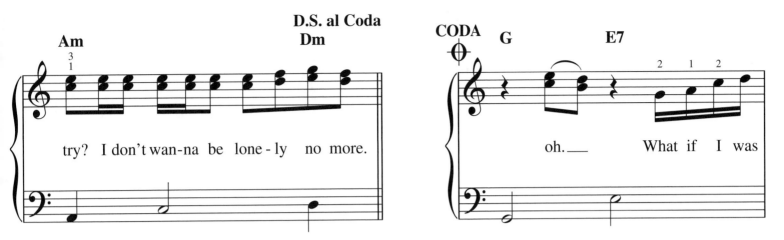

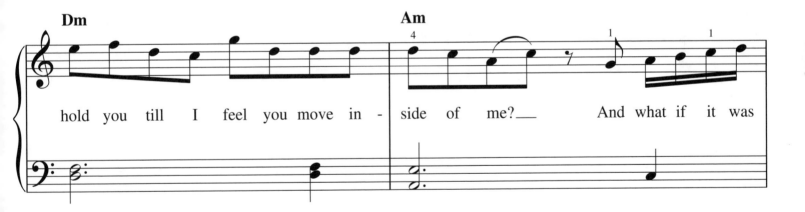

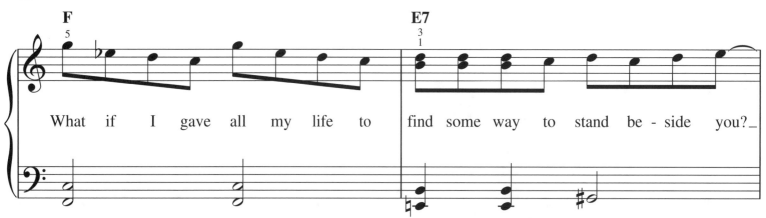

What if I gave all my life to find some way to stand be - side you?

I don't wan-na be lone - ly no more. I don't wan-na have to pay for this.

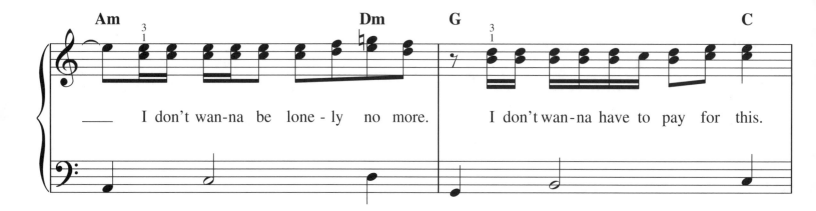

I don't wan-na know the lov - er at my door is just an-oth-er heart-ache on my

list. I don't wan-na be an - gry no more. But you know I could nev-er stand for this.

So when you tell me that you love me, know for sure. I don't wan-na be lone-ly an-y-more.

Oh,_____ oh,_____ oh,____ oh._____

____ Oh,_____ oh,_____

1.
I don't wan-na be lone-ly an-y-more.

2.
I don't wan-na be lone-ly an-y-more.____

SINCE U BEEN GONE

Words and Music by MARTIN SANDBERG
and LUKASZ GOTTWALD

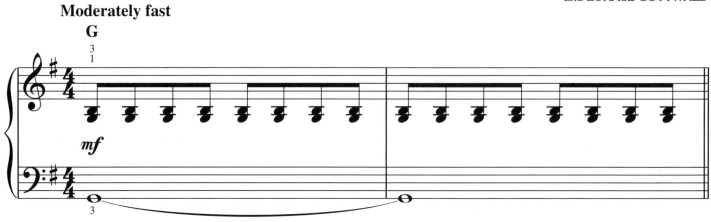

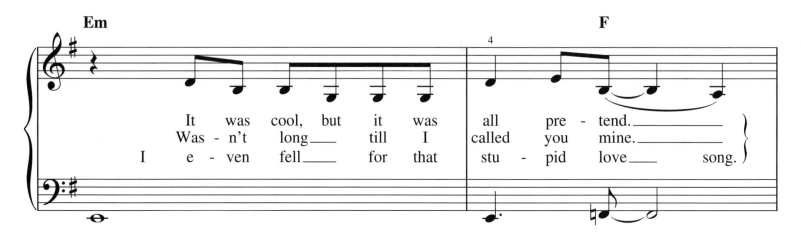

Here's the thing: we start - ed out friends.
You ded - i - cat - ed, you took the time.
How can I put it? You put me on.

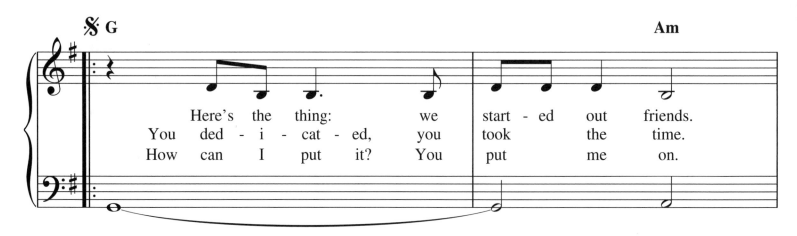

It was cool, but it was all pre - tend._____
Was - n't long____ till I called you mine._____
I e - ven fell____ for that stu - pid love____ song.

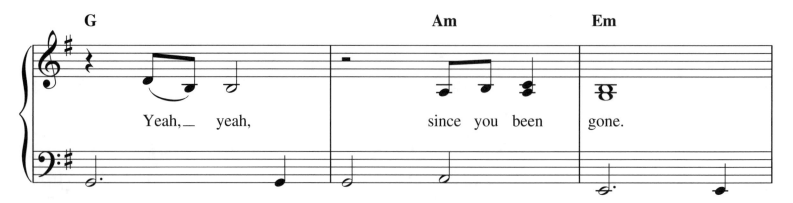

Yeah,___ yeah, since you been gone.

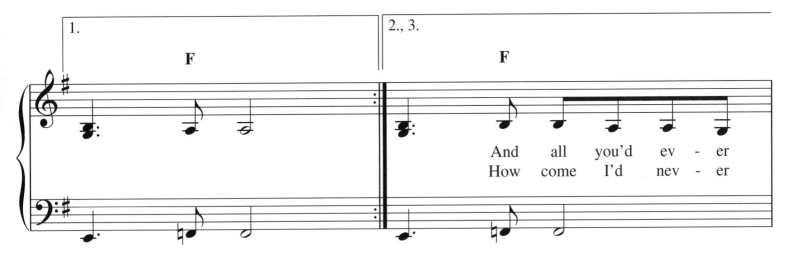

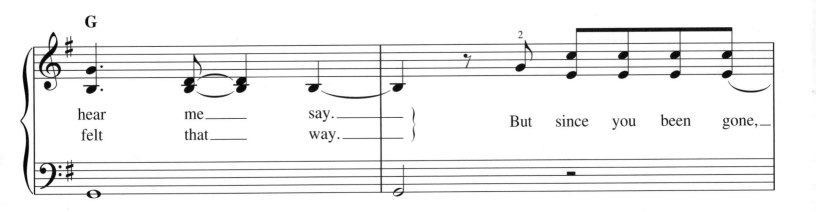

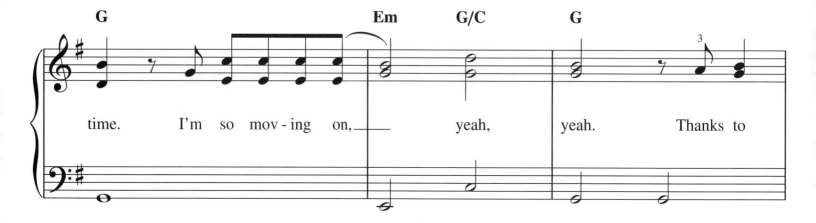

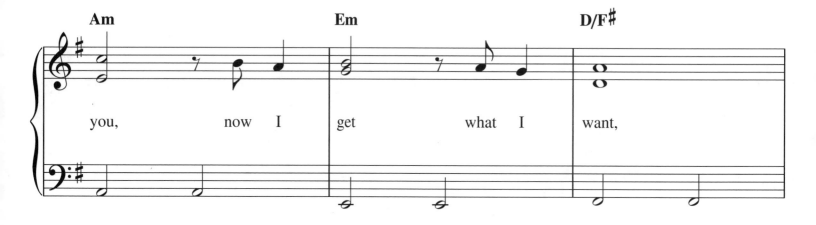

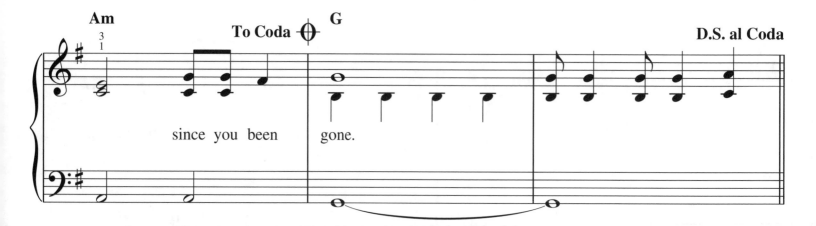

CODA

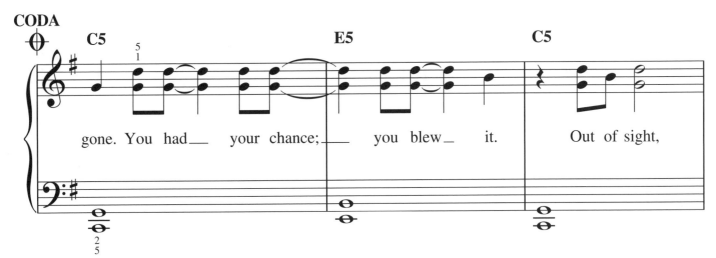

gone. You had___ your chance;___ you blew___ it.   Out of sight,

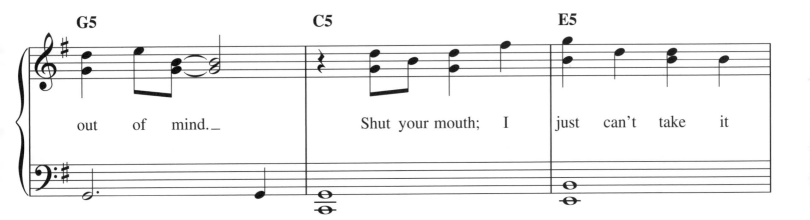

out of mind.___   Shut your mouth; I   just can't take it

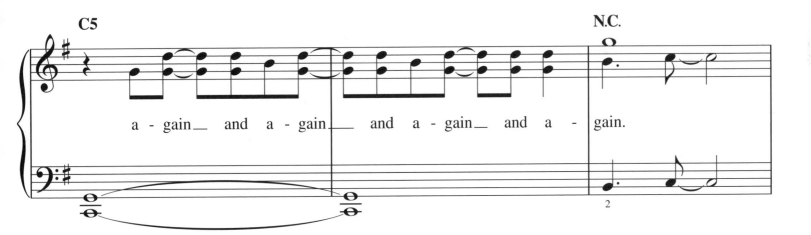

a - gain___ and a - gain___ and a - gain___ and a - gain.

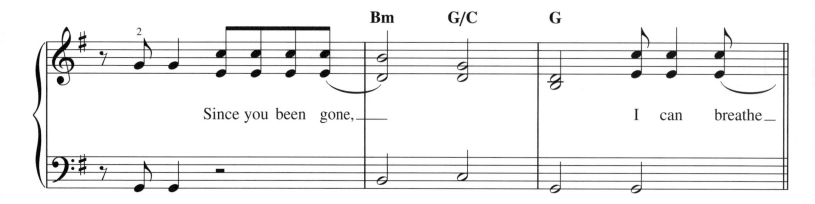

Since you been gone,_____ I can breathe__

_____ for the first time. I'm so mov-ing on,_____ yeah,

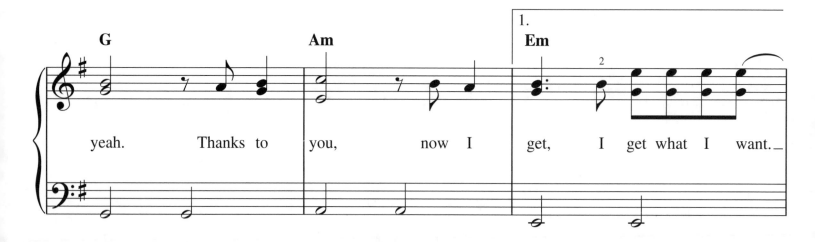

yeah. Thanks to you, now I get, I get what I want.__

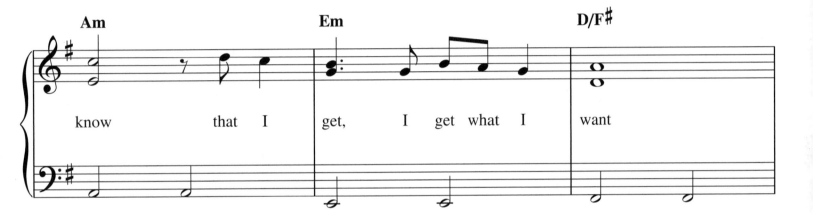

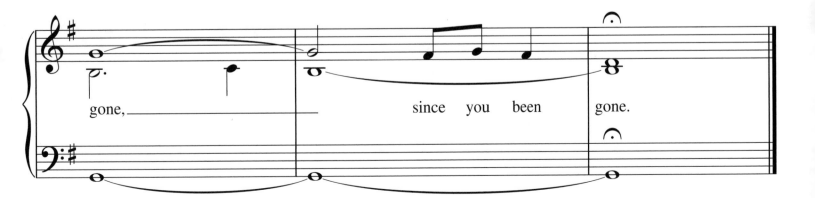

TRUE

Words and Music by RYAN CABRERA,
JIMMY HARRY and SHEPPARD SOLOMON

Moderately

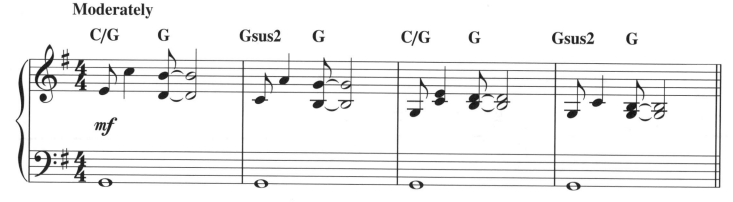

I won't talk.__ I won't breathe.__ I won't move__ 'til you

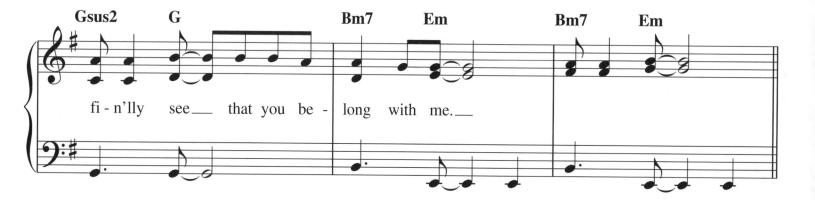

fi - n'lly see__ that you be - long with me.__

You might think__ I don't look,__ but deep in - side__ the cor -
You don't know__ what you do__ ev -'ry time__ you walk__

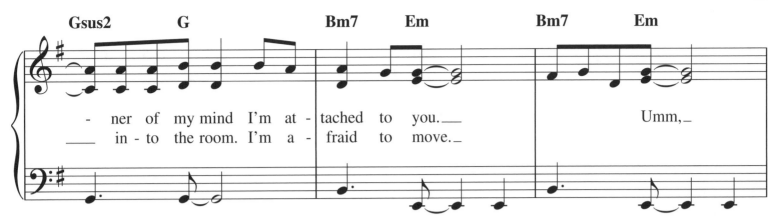

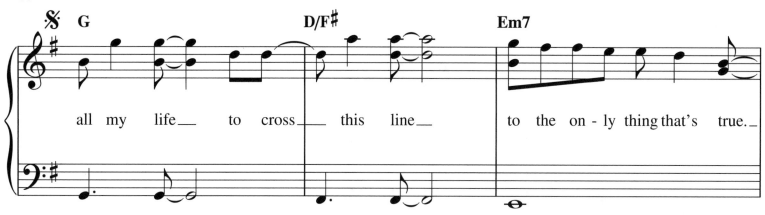

all my life___ to cross___ this line___ to the on - ly thing that's true.___

___ So I will___ not hide.___ It's time___ to try___

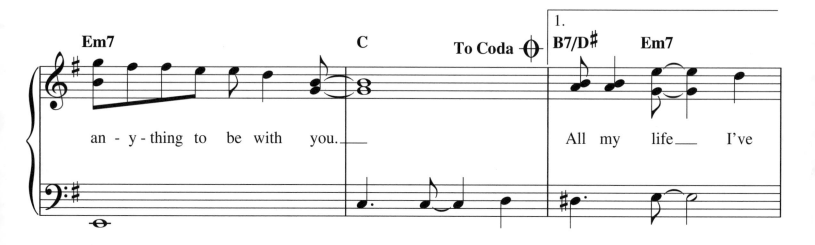

an - y - thing to be with you.___ All my life___ I've

wait - ed, this is true.___

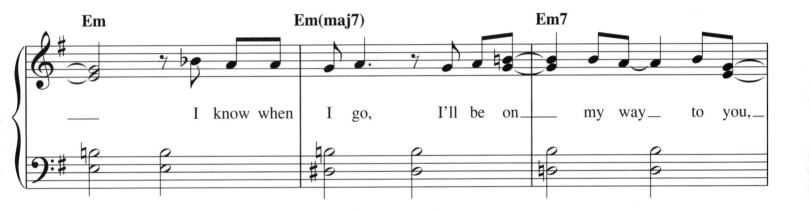

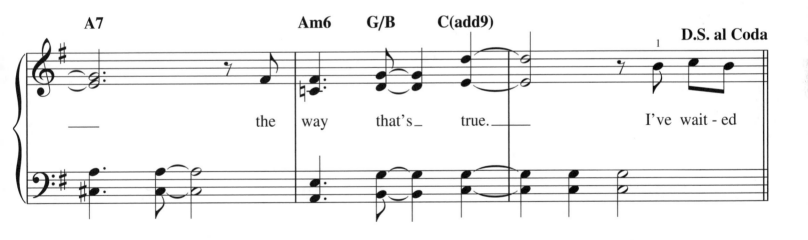

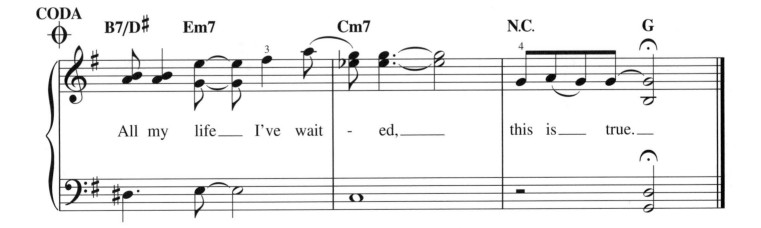

WHITE HOUSES

Words and Music by VANESSA CARLTON
and STEPHAN JENKINS

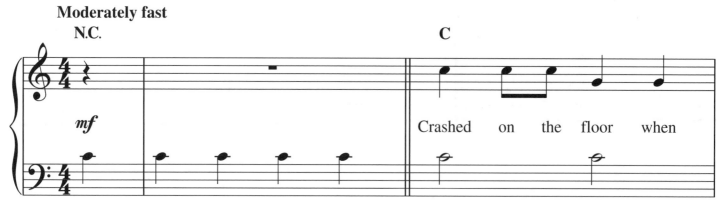

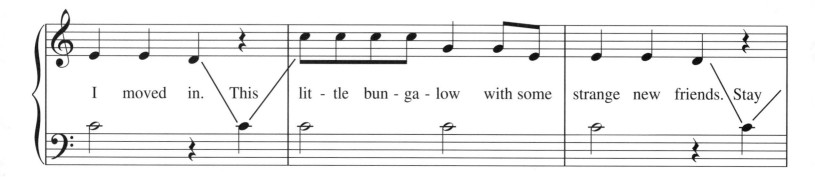

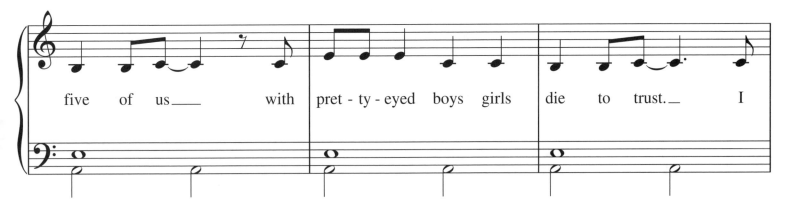

five of us___ with pret - ty - eyed boys girls die to trust.___ I

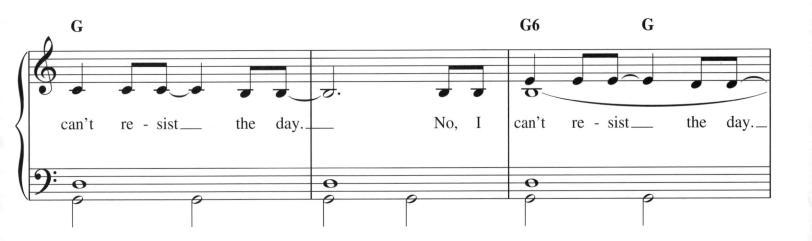

G

can't re - sist___ the day.___ No, I can't re - sist___ the day.___

G6 **G**

C

___ And Jen - ny screams out and it's no pose, 'cause

when she danc - es she goes and goes. And beer through the nose on an

C/B

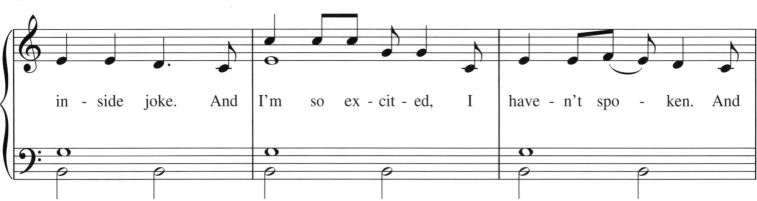

in - side joke. And I'm so ex - cit - ed, I have - n't spo - ken. And

Am

she's so pret - ty and she's so sure.__ May - be I'm more clev - er than a

                              Gsus   **G**

girl like her.__ Sum-mer's all__ in bloom. The

Gsus   **G**   **F5**

sum-mer's end - ing soon. It's al - right__ and it's nice__

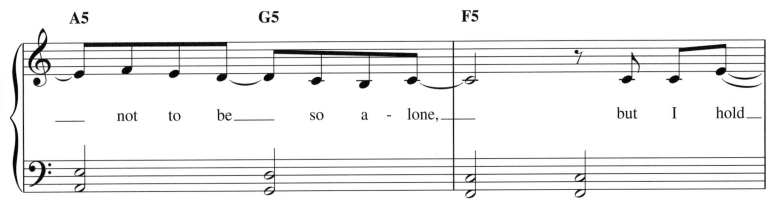

not to be so a - lone, but I hold

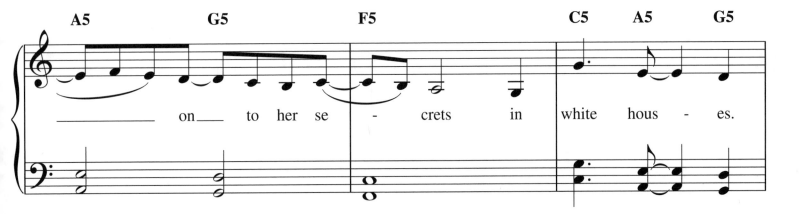

on to her se - crets in white hous - es.

May - be I'm a lit - tle bit o - ver my head. I

come un - done at the things he said. And he's so fun - ny in his

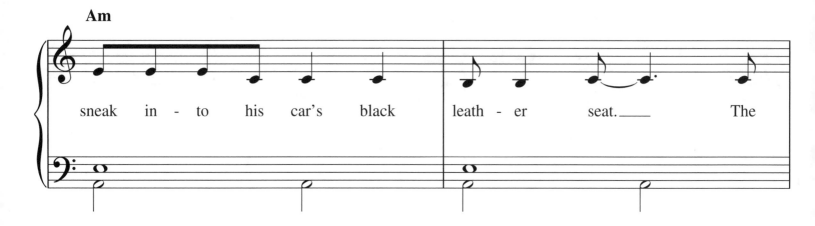

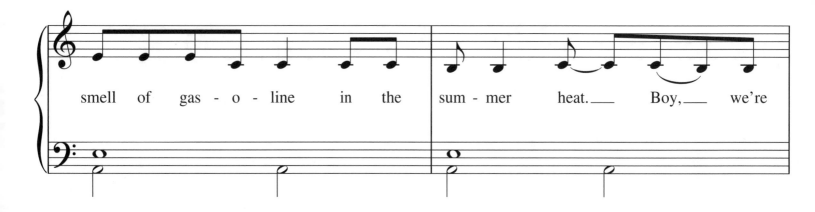

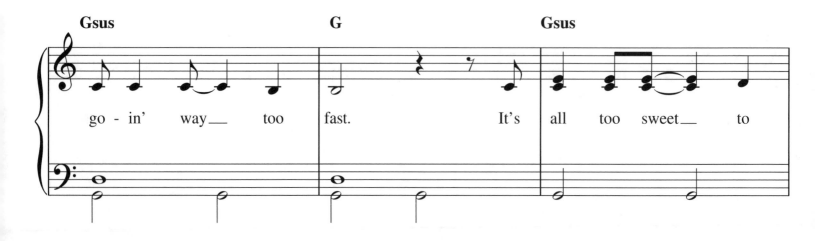

last. It's al - right ____ and I put ____ / and I will ____

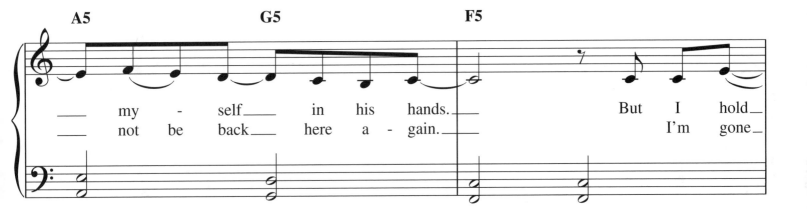

____ my - self ____ in his hands. ____ But I hold ____
____ not be back ____ here a - gain. ____ I'm gone ____

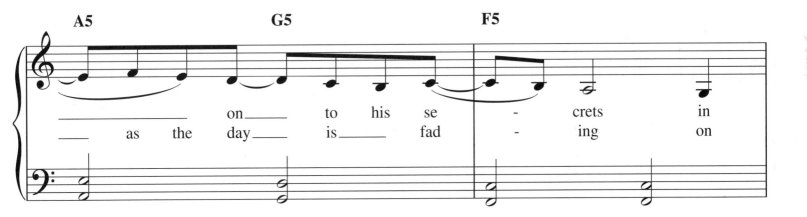

____ on ____ to his se - crets in
____ as the day ____ is ____ fad - ing on

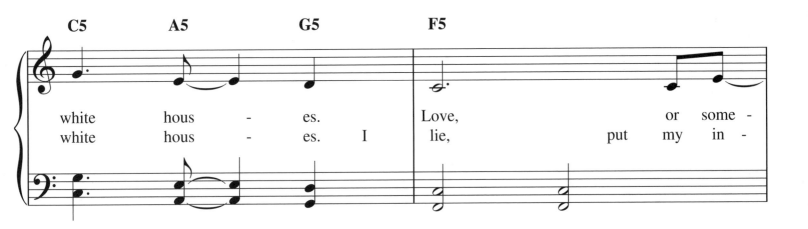

white hous - es. Love, or some -
white hous - es. I lie, put my in -

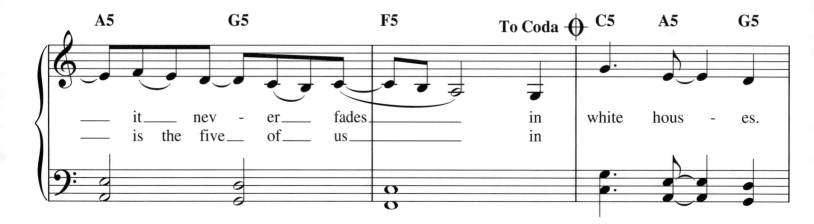

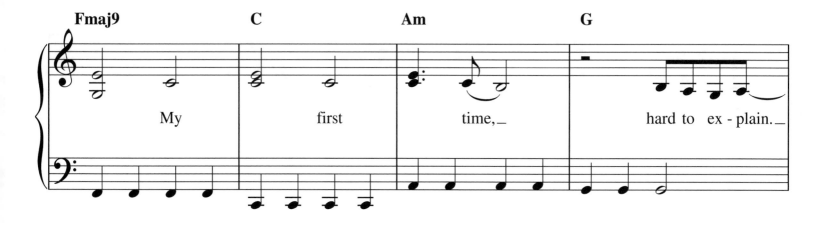

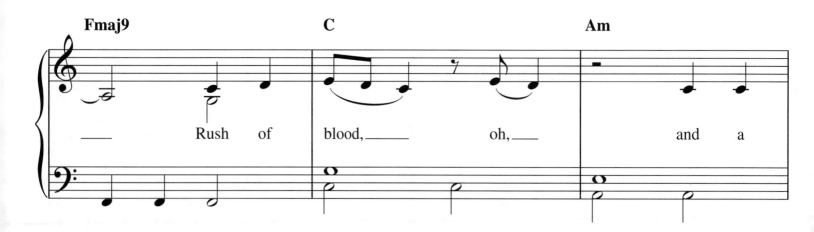

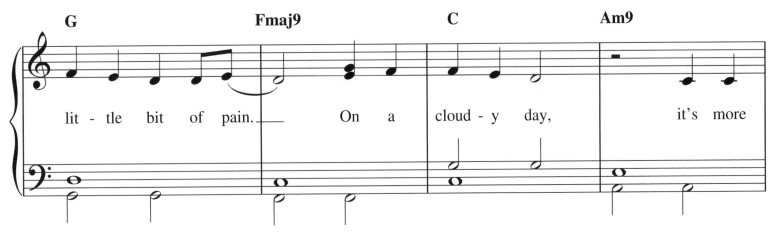

May - be you were all fast - er than me. We

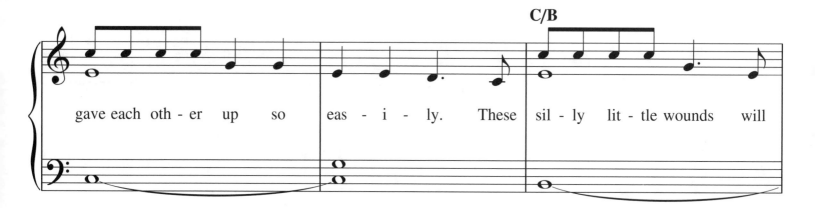

gave each oth - er up so eas - i - ly. These sil - ly lit - tle wounds will

nev - er mend. I feel so far from where I've been._ So I go__

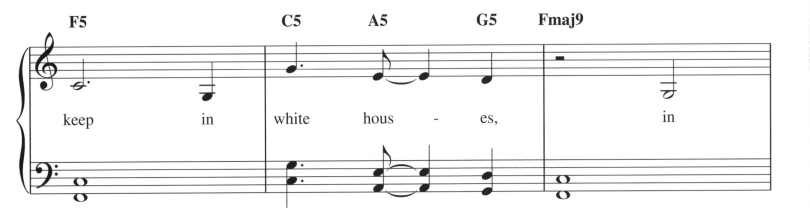

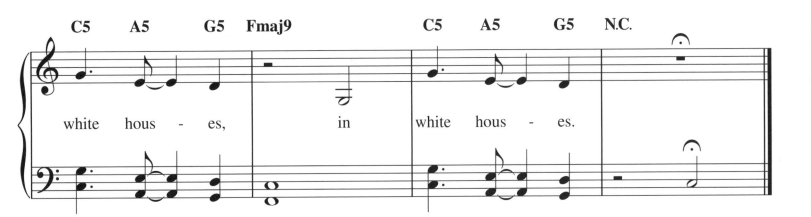

SOMEWHERE ONLY WE KNOW

Words and Music by TIM RICE-OXLEY,
RICHARD HUGHES and TOM CHAPLIN

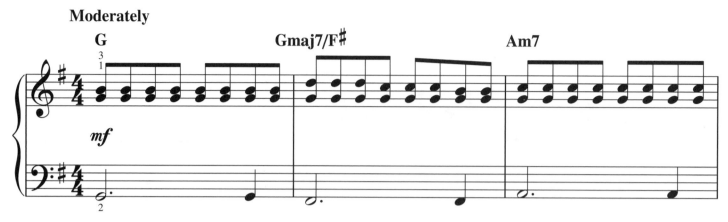

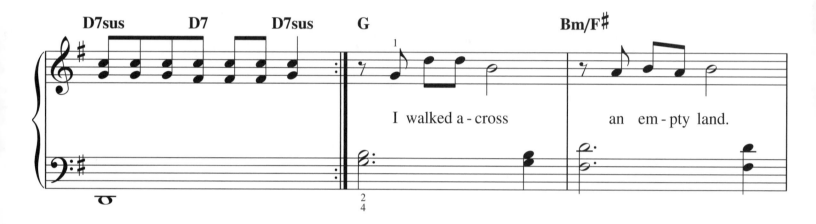

Oh, sim-ple thing, where have you gone? I'm get-ting old and I need

some-thing to re - ly on. So tell me when you're gon-na let me in.

I'm get-ting tired and I need some-where to be - gin.___ I came a-cross

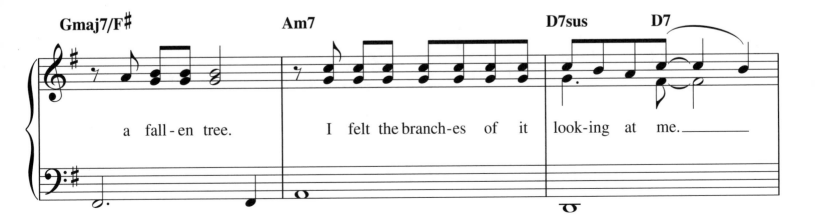

a fall-en tree. I felt the branch-es of it look-ing at me.___

Is this the place we used to love? Is this the place that I've been

dream-ing of?_____ Oh, sim-ple thing, where have you gone?

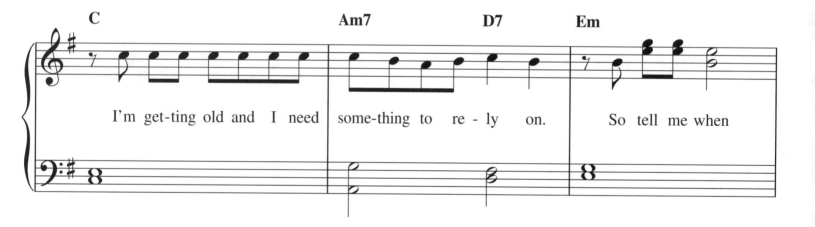

I'm get-ting old and I need some-thing to re - ly on. So tell me when

you're gon-na let me in. I'm get-ting tired and I need some-where to be - gin.___

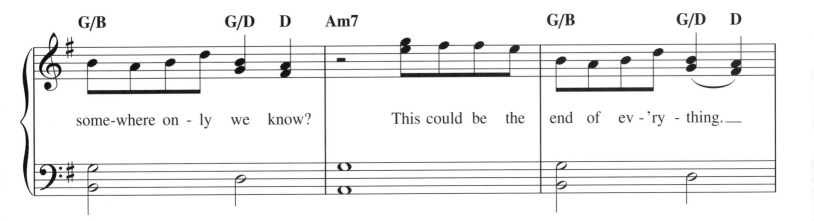

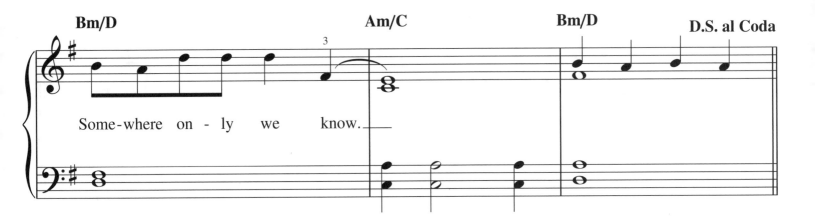

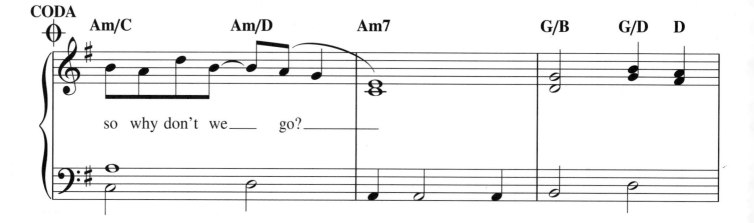

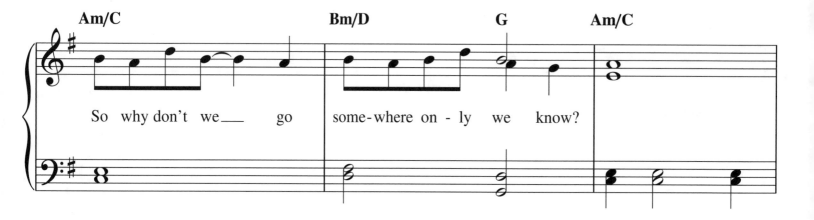

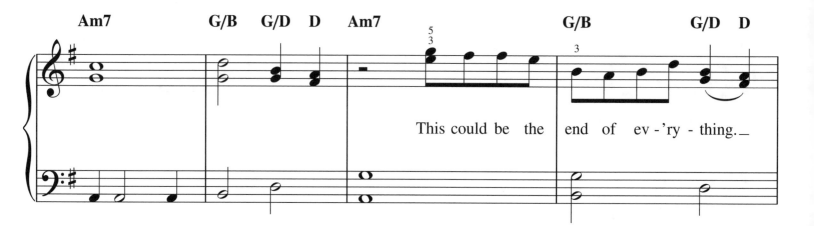

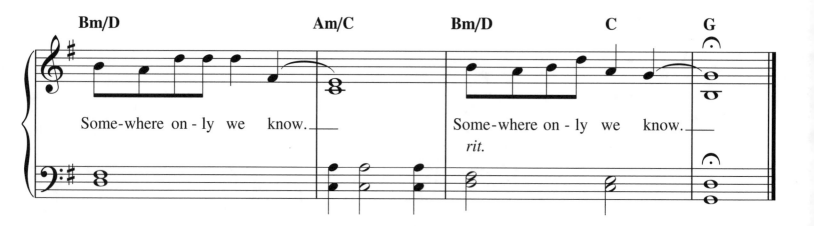

It's Easy to Play Your Favorite Songs with Hal Leonard Easy Piano Books

The Best Songs Ever
Over 70 all-time favorite songs, including: All I Ask of You • Body and Soul • Call Me Irresponsible • Crazy • Edelweiss • Fly Me to the Moon • The Girl from Ipanema • Here's That Rainy Day • Imagine • Let It Be • Longer • Moon River • Moonlight in Vermont • People • Satin Doll • Save the Best for Last • Somewhere Out There • Stormy Weather • Strangers in the Night • Tears in Heaven • Unchained Melody • Unforgettable • The Way We Were • What a Wonderful World • When I Fall in Love • and more
00359223 ....$19.95

Broadway Songs for Kids
19 songs, including: Be Kind to Your Parents • Beauty and the Beast • Castle on a Cloud • Gary, Indiana • I Won't Grow Up • It's the Hard-Knock Life • Little People • Tomorrow • and more.
00310354 ....$12.95

Contemporary Christian Songs
15 songs, including: Friends • Great Is the Lord • He Who Began a Good Work in You • Holy, Holy • Hosanna • How Majestic Is Your Name • I Will Be Here • In the Name of the Lord • Lamb of Glory • Lord of All • Love in Any Language • Love Will Be Our Home • O Magnify the Lord • Oh Lord, You're Beautiful • Thy Word.
00222501 ....$8.95

Contemporary Love Songs
27 heart-felt favorites: Breathe • Forever in Love • Here and Now • I Will Remember You • I'll Be • Just the Way You Are • My Heart Will Go On • Ribbon in the Sky • Tears in Heaven • Through the Years • Valentine • Vision of Love • When She Loved Me • You'll Be in My Heart • and more.
00310655 ....$12.95

Favorite Ballads of the '80s and '90s
25 contemporary ballads, including: Can You Feel the Love Tonight • Eternal Flame • From a Distance • Glory of Love • Hero • I Just Called to Say I Love You • I Swear • Just Once • Lady in Red • My Heart Will Go On • (I've Had) The Time of My Life • Up Where We Belong • The Way We Were • Wonderful Tonight • and more.
00310795 ....$10.95

God Bless America® & Other American Inspirations
20 American classics: America, the Beautiful • Battle Hymn of the Republic • God Bless America • My Country, 'Tis of Thee • The Star Spangled Banner • Stars and Stripes Forever • This Is My Country • This Land Is Your Land • United We Stand • and more.
00310826...$10.95

Irish Favorites
From sentimental favorites to happy-go-lucky singalongs, this songbook celebrates the Irish cultural heritage of music. 30 songs: Danny Boy (Londonderry Air) • The Girl I Left Behind Me • It's a Long, Long Way to Tipperary • Killarney • My Wild Irish Rose • Too-ra-loo-ra-loo-ral, That's An Irish Lullabye • When Irish Eyes Are Smiling • and more!
00110011...$9.95

The Best of Andrew Lloyd Webber
11 of his best, arranged by Bill Boyd. Includes: All I Ask of You • Don't Cry for Me Argentina • I Don't Know How to Love Him • Memory • Mr. Mistoffelees • The Music of the Night • The Phantom of the Opera • Pie Jesu • Superstar • Take That Look off Your Face • Think of Me.
00290333..$12.95

Movie Favorites
20 songs, including: Beauty and the Beast • Endless Love • The Rainbow Connection • Somewhere Out There • Theme from "Ordinary People" • Unchained Melody • Under the Sea • What a Wonderful World • and more.
00222551..$9.95

The Really Big Book of Children's Songs
63 kids' hits: Alley Cat Song • Any Dream Will Do • Circle of Life • The Grouch Song • Hakuna Matata • I Won't Grow Up • Kum-Ba-Yah • Monster Mash • My Favorite Things • Sesame Street Theme • Winnie the Pooh • You've Got a Friend in Me • and more.
00310372...$15.95

1203

EASY PIANO CD PLAY-ALONGS
Orchestrated arrangements with you as the soloist!

This series lets you play along with great accompaniments to songs you know and love! Each book comes with a CD of complete professional performances and includes matching custom arrangements in Easy Piano format. With these books you can: Listen to complete professional performances of each of the songs; Play the Easy Piano arrangements along with the performances; Sing along with the recordings; Play the Easy Piano arrangements as solos, without the CD.

GREAT JAZZ STANDARDS – VOLUME 1
Bewitched • Do Nothin' Till You Hear from Me • Don't Get Around Much Anymore • How Deep Is the Ocean • I'm Beginning to See the Light • It Might As Well Be Spring • My Funny Valentine • Satin Doll • Stardust • That Old Black Magic.
00310916 Easy Piano $14.95

FAVORITE CLASSICAL THEMES – VOLUME 2
Bach: Air on the G String • Beethoven: Symphony No. 5, Excerpt • Bizet: Habanera • Franck: Panis Angelicus • Gounod: Ave Maria • Grieg: Morning • Handel: Hallelujah Chorus • Humperdinck: Evening Prayer • Mozart: Piano Concerto No. 21, Excerpt • Offenbach: Can Can • Pachelbel: Canon • Strauss: Emperor Waltz • Tchaikovsky: Waltz of the Flowers.
00310921 Easy Piano $14.95

BROADWAY FAVORITES – VOLUME 3
All I Ask of You • Beauty and the Beast • Bring Him Home • Cabaret • Close Every Door • I've Never Been in Love Before • If I Loved You • Memory • My Favorite Things • Some Enchanted Evening.
00310915 Easy Piano $14.95

ADULT CONTEMPORARY HITS – VOLUME 4
Amazed • Angel • Breathe • I Don't Want to Wait • I Hope You Dance • I Will Remember You • I'll Be • It's Your Love • The Power of Love • You'll Be in My Heart.
00310919 Easy Piano $14.95

HIT POP/ROCK BALLADS – VOLUME 5
Don't Let the Sun Go Down on Me • From a Distance • I Can't Make You Love Me • I'll Be There • Imagine • In My Room • My Heart Will Go On • Rainy Days and Mondays • Total Eclipse of the Heart • A Whiter Shade of Pale.
00310917 Easy Piano $14.95

Disney characters and artwork © Disney Enterprises, Inc.

Prices, contents and availability subject to change without notice.

LOVE SONG FAVORITES – VOLUME 6
Fields of Gold • I Honestly Love You • If • Lady in Red • More Than Words • Save the Best for Last • Three Times a Lady • Up Where We Belong • We've Only Just Begun • You Are So Beautiful.
00310918 Easy Piano $14.95

O HOLY NIGHT – VOLUME 7
Angels We Have Heard on High • Deck the Hall • Ding Dong! Merrily on High! • Go, Tell It on the Mountain • God Rest Ye Merry, Gentlemen • Good Christian Men, Rejoice • It Came upon the Midnight Clear • Jingle Bells • Lo, How a Rose E'er Blooming • O Come, All Ye Faithful • O Come, O Come Immanuel • O Holy Night • Once in Royal David's City • Silent Night • What Child Is This?
00310920 Easy Piano $14.95

A CHRISTIAN WEDDING – VOLUME 8
Cherish the Treasure • Commitment Song • How Beautiful • I Will Be Here • In This Very Room • The Lord's Prayer • Love Will Be Our Home • Parent's Prayer • This Is the Day • The Wedding.
00311104 Easy Piano $14.95

COUNTRY BALLADS – VOLUME 9
Always on My Mind • Could I Have This Dance • Crazy • Crying • Forever and Ever, Amen • He Stopped Loving Her Today • I Can Love You Like That • The Keeper of the Stars • Release Me • When You Say Nothing at All.
00311105 Easy Piano $14.95

MOVIE GREATS – VOLUME 10
And All That Jazz • Chariots of Fire • Come What May • Forrest Gump • I Finally Found Someone • Iris • Mission: Impossible Theme • Tears in Heaven • There You'll Be • A Wink and a Smile.
00311106 Easy Piano $14.95

DISNEY BLOCKBUSTERS – VOLUME 11
Be Our Guest • Can You Feel the Love Tonight • Go the Distance • Look Through My Eyes • Reflection • Two Worlds • Under the Sea • A Whole New World • Written in the Stars • You've Got a Friend in Me.
00311107 Easy Piano $14.95

CHRISTMAS FAVORITES – VOLUME 12
Blue Christmas • Frosty the Snow Man • Here Comes Santa Claus • A Holly Jolly Christmas • Home for the Holidays • I'll Be Home for Christmas • Merry Christmas, Darling • Mistletoe and Holly • Silver Bells • Wonderful Christmastime.
00311257 Easy Piano $14.95

CHILDREN'S SONGS – VOLUME 13
Any Dream Will Do • Do-Re-Mi • It's a Small World • Linus and Lucy • The Rainbow Connection • Splish Splash • This Land Is Your Land • Winnie the Pooh • Yellow Submarine • Zip-A-Dee-Doo-Dah.
00311258 Easy Piano $14.95

CHILDREN'S FAVORITES – VOLUME 14
Alphabet Song • Down by the Station • Eensy Weensy Spider • Frere Jacques • Home on the Range • I've Been Working on the Railroad • Kum Ba Yah • The Muffin Man • My Bonnie Lies over the Ocean • Oh! Susanna • Old MacDonald • Row, Row, Row Your Boat • She'll Be Comin' 'Round the Mountain • This Old Man • Yankee Doodle.
00311259 Easy Piano $14.95

DISNEY'S BEST – VOLUME 15
Beauty and the Beast • Bibbidi-Bobbidi-Boo • Chim Chim Cher-ee • Colors of the Wind • Friend Like Me • Hakuna Matata • Part of Your World • Someday • When She Loved Me • You'll Be in My Heart.
00311260 Easy Piano $14.95

LENNON & McCARTNEY – VOLUME 16
Eleanor Rigby • Hey Jude • The Long and Winding Road • Love Me Do • Lucy in the Sky with Diamonds • Nowhere Man • Strawberry Fields Forever • Yesterday.
00311262 Easy Piano $14.95

FOR MORE INFORMATION, SEE YOUR LOCAL MUSIC DEALER, OR WRITE TO:

HAL•LEONARD® CORPORATION
7777 W. BLUEMOUND RD. P.O. BOX 13819 MILWAUKEE, WI 53213

www.halleonard.com

0605